THE WATERMILL SAGA

READ IT ENJOY IT

SHARE IT

Ed Miller

Somewhere in Poland, between Lvov and Warsaw, in an idyllic valley, sits the town of Watermill, with its story, its castle and its crows, black as the night.

THE WATERMILL SAGA

HISTORY, MYSTERY, INTRIGUE OF THE SHLOSS!

ED MILLER

Library of Congress Control Number: 2013903481

ISBN:	Softcover	978-1-4836-0036-9
	Ebook	978-1-4836-0037-6

This book was printed in the United States of America.

Rev. date: 04/30/2013

To order additional copies of this book, contact:
Xlibris Corporation
1-888-795-4274
www.Xlibris.com
Orders@Xlibris.com
130591

Contents

The Castle of Watermill

I

Preface

NO ONE WOULD have heard of Watermill or even Pilski, unless they lived there or passed through, on the way to somewhere else in the vast countryside of Poland. These places were not of much importance like Warsaw, Lvov or Crackow, known as centers of riches, culture, religion and power. Smaller ones like Przemysl, or a town like Dobromil had long, peaceful and local histories, a life of its own, that included the "Holocaust"

EM

Acknowledgement: Undying gratitude for friendship and superb editing skill . . .
Ms. Terry Riccardi, associate in Queens UFT Creative Writing Class.

The Castle of Watermill

SOMEWHERE, IT IS written that on the thirty-third day of the Omer, Lag B'Omer in the Jewish calendar, the boys and girls of Watermill make the annual pilgrimage up to the Shloss, the Castle. On a hilltop overlooking the beautiful valley it stands, majestic and solemn and fearful. As long as memory allows, the castle was said to be haunted, but what castle isn't? Only by daylight would anyone dare to climb the broken stone path, past the rusty iron gates. The moss and ivy crawled unimpeded up the heavy gray masonry almost to the turrets that once boasted a defending army of knights. For this small Polish town to have such an edifice was quite unique and all the people of Watermill were truly proud of it. The children crept up as close as they dared to the huge hewn oaken doors, once rich in color, now a dismal gray, almost the color of the stone that surrounded them.

Benny, who led the pack of children, not the biggest or the oldest but the bravest, stood at the fore scanning the huge edifice before him. He reached down, found a rock in the path and heaved it with all his might. Even those who were next to him were startled at the crack that split the air when the oaken door was struck. A flock of crows, disturbed by the intrusion, exited their perches in the windows above, with the fluttering of their black wings and their fearsome screams. All of the children turned and ran. All except Benny, who stood there delighted in his mischief. Below, at the bottom of the path, the other children looked back to see the birds returning to their nests, settling back in the window ledges where once there was life and light. Many people have reported that on the night of the fast day Tisha B'Av, they could see a light, a candle burning in the window of the tower, high above, in the Shloss, especially clear from the Jewish section of town. A flickering light like a memorial, Yahrzeit candle. Many of the medieval cities boasted a castle, but a town like Watermill was an exception. It was built when the peasants were serfs and what little commerce there was transpired at the Thursday fair. In those days, long forgotten, there were few Jews in Watermill, having settled there after falling in love with the beautiful valley, the pastoral peace of the surrounding hills, guarded by the majestic Carpathian Mountains that hugged the sky. Why shouldn't they settle into this idyllic setting, especially since the Baron Pilsudski, the owner of this paradise, welcomed the Jews?

It is true that he was a devout Catholic, a G-d fearing Christian, but he came to know the Jews as industrious and honest artisans with skills that his serfs found hard to master. Of course the law of the land decreed segregation and being a loyal servant of the king, it was so in his domain. The Baron seldom came to town, preferring to hold court in the Shloss. It was during such a session that he met Shlomo, a small Jew, a tailor by trade, who had migrated with his wife from the neighboring city, Pilski. "P-p-pilski," Shlomo used to stutter, "W-w-as H-hell!" Being the only Cathedral city in that area of Poland made it a powerful and important seat of government. It was not the King who governed there but the Bishop, and any edict made by him automatically became law. The Bishop was a very tall gaunt man and his red eyes burned with a venomous hatred for the Jews. How anyone of the Jewish faith could survive in that city was beyond belief. So Shlomo, although poor but wise, like his namesake, Solomon, decided not to stay in Hell. To walk the twenty or so miles to Watermill should have taken maybe five hours but his wife was heavy with child and the cart filled with the tools of his trade and their meager possessions becoming heavier by the mile, made the trip take all day. Shlomo turned to his wife, stopping periodically for her to catch up to him and said, N-n-n-nu! S-s-s-surahlah, our good G-G-G—d has b-brought us s-s-safely this far, w-w-w-we will s-s-s-soon s-s-see our n-n-n-new h-h-home!" Neither seemed to notice that the street that lay ahead only boasted five houses, two on one side of the street and three on the other. Panting with exhaustion, Sarah could hardly express her joy at seeing the end of their journey. A little further, with G-d's help and she would finally get to rest, her bundle becoming more restless every step. The sun was low on the horizon and Shlomo stopped, setting his cart at the edge of the narrow rutted road. "S-S-Suralah!" he said softly, "W-w-we'll s-s-stop for a m-m-m-minute. It's t-t-time f-f-for the evening p-p-p-prayer, s-s-s-so you g-go r-r-r-rest against the w-w-w-wagon. Shlomo then turned to the East and proceeded to pray. Not just the evening prayer but for the safety and success in their new home. The strangest thing was that Shlomo never stuttered when he prayed; only when he spoke Polish or Yiddish did he have this affliction. Sarah was becoming impatient, so with the one word, "Nu!" from her, Shlomo finished and they were on their way, descending into Watermill their new home. From the hills behind them came the sound of horses' hooves beating in cadence on the hard dirt road. As fast as they could they moved to the skirt of the road. The sound increased as four horsemen raced into view, passed them and disappeared down the road ahead of them. In the din of the horses Shlomo could hardly make out the words, "something Zhid!" obviously not complimentary, considering the spit that he was removing from his face. "Thank you, G-d," he thought, "for the very nice welcome." Soon the dust settled and they continued on their way to the houses in the distance.

The thatched roofed houses were set on either side of the street. Two were Polish, with the crucifix nailed to the door lintel. One was a makeshift chapel of the town priest before it was replaced by the stone church to be built in the future. The Father seldom used it for confession, as he would travel around the parish holding Mass at the different fiefdoms. The other "house" held services, too; however the madame and her girls never came out, while the patrons were in and out all day and night. Across the street at a small distance away were the Jewish houses. If there were any religious symbols on them they were not advertised. One was a "general store' where all sorts of household items were sold. Well, actually, given on credit. With the good graces of the serf's owners, and Muzhiks, in time they were paid for. The second Jewish house was occupied by the metal smith, a blacksmith, a tall husky man who wielded his hammer as it were a feather that made the metal he worked on practically jump into the shapes he wanted. His anvil would ring from dawn to dusk like the bell in the cathedral tower in Pilski.

The third house was a tavern. Jews were not supposed to own any taverns but this law was often overlooked. The talented vintner was able to brew cheap vodka, sometimes flavored with fruit juices. He made some vintage brandy, called Shlivovitz, which had the magic of instantly warming one on the coldest freezing night, from the top of the head to the tips of one's toes. As the two weary travelers approached the houses they could see the four horses tied up in front of the tavern. A strange feeling of fear gripped Shlomo's heart but they moved on anyway. Cautiously, he approached the plain wooden door. It creaked as his travel-weary arm pulled it open. Barely inside, he removed his hat, which is something Jewish custom forbids, but as a sign of humility before the Christians, he did it. He cleared his throat and mumbled, "Excuse m-m-me." One of the horsemen turned and seeing this poor example of a human being, picked up a copper kopek from the counter and flung it at him as one throws alms to a beggar. The bartender, recognizing a fellow Jew, signed with his head for Shlomo to please wait outside. In a few minutes, Nathan, the taverner, was signaling for Sarah and Shlomo to follow him to the rear of the house. Nathan's wife and two little children came to the back door when Nathan knocked and seeing Sarah's condition, grabbed her two hands and ushered her into the back room. In minutes, Naomi set the table with food and drink, simple fare, it is true, but more than a wayfarer could expect.

The two women became friends almost immediately. Nathan had to excuse himself, running around to the front of the tavern to service the horsemen, who were really knights to the Baron. Now they were relegated to the job of policemen, since an accord was signed among all of the surrounding manors and fiefdoms and their weapons and armor were no longer needed. Because the attic was used to store necessities of the trade and the cellar was used for distilling and storing the wines and liquors, space was made in the small room for both Sarah and Shlomo as if by magic. Soon after the bar closed, Nathan reappeared and sat down to eat his supper meal of course bread and soup. The children were asleep in the corner of the room; curled up like kittens on the burlap mattress they called a bed. Shlomo let Nathan do all the talking; it was easier that way.

Before opening the tavern in Watermill, Nathan and his young wife had tried to start a business in Pilski but the edicts of the Bishop made it impossible. "S-s-s-so what's n-n-new?" stuttered Shlomo. "Only twenty miles and it's a different world!" said Nathan. Well, it was still Poland, it was still dangerous to be a Jew but as Nathan put it, "With the

Creator's help . . ." He didn't have to finish. Everyone knew! The dishes were cleared, the lamps extinguished and the adults lay down on sacks that covered the dirt floor, to sleep. All was quiet except for the crickets. The black night covered everything like a blanket. The shriek that came from Sarah's mouth was inhuman. Everyone was awakened immediately. All Sarah could say was, "Oy! Oy! Oy! G-d in Heaven!" She felt that she was being torn apart. Fortunately, Naomi had had two babies so she knew what to do. The children were sent up to the attic, out of the way. The fire in the fireplace was rekindled and water was set to boil. Shlomo stood over his beloved wife, frightened to death but concealing it from Sarah. He stroked her damp forehead gently, silently praying, pleading with the Almighty to help his poor wife. Naomi ordered her husband, Nathan, to tear up the linen sheets that she handed him. All of a sudden Sarah was soaking wet. Shlomo gasped at the sight. At each cry he squeezed her hand. Nathan's strips kept coming as Shlomo kept wiping her brow and the water around her bottom. "Gevalt!" she screamed. Naomi tried to comfort her. "The first child is the hardest!" she said. There was no midwife, no doctor. Naomi had to be both. The birthing was complicated by the position of the baby. It was coming feet first, the worst of complications. Sarah stopped screaming. She seemed to doze off. The men were relieved that she was resting but Naomi knew better. Sarah awoke with a shriek that would have startled the devil in Hell. Then, suddenly, with a terrible flush of blood and pain the baby squeezed out into the sheets that Naomi had prepared. Immediately the infant was wrapped in the course linen and the umbilical cord was cut and tied and the baby was washed. The men stood there amazed at the efficient way that Naomi had taken charge. Sarah's body was completely exhausted and limp. She just laid there, her throat hurt from screaming, her body hurt from the pain of birth. She could hardly whisper the question, "NU?" Naomi smiled down at her and whispered, "A maydele!" a little girl. Before she fell asleep, Sarah said, "We'll call her 'Chayele,' the little beast that was inside me." Naomi smiled and said, "Yes, Chayele, for the little life you've brought forth!"

No one knew the damage the baby Chayele had suffered in her voyage into this cruel world. Only a few days later she died, leaving everyone devastated. For a whole week the tavern was closed. A small plot of ground behind the tavern was designated as the Jewish cemetery. The general store provided the small planks of pine for the coffin. There was no quorum of Jews as prescribed by law. The handful that was there in Watermill attended the rites. It was the first death, the only Jewish death in this town. A wooden fence was erected to protect the grave. The notice of death posted on the door of the tavern was respected by the peasants and horsemen alike. When Baron Pilsudski heard about the death, he sent a message of condolence. The week of mourning passed and it was time to return to day-to-day occupation. The hospitality of Nathan and Naomi continued while Sarah convalesced but Shlomo started immediately to set about getting a house built. It certainly was not a large house, as large as the tavern or even the general store or the metal smith. After all, what room does a tailor need for his needles and thread and pins, thimble and measuring tape?

The house across the street, with the big cross on the door, was now occupied by the town priest, semi-retired. With the influx of merchants and artisans from the city, the town of Watermill began to grow. Actually it grew in the direction of the Shloss, under whose protection it lay. A church was being built, funded by the Bishop and a new, younger priest was going to be installed. The old priest was neutral as far as the Jews were concerned. They didn't interfere with his giving the Holy Sacraments and he didn't interfere with them. But what the relationship was going to be with the new priest, no one knew. Everyone went about their business, giving honest service and keeping the peace. The peasants attended the weekly fairs, which soon became known throughout the region.

Two years passed and Shlomo became well known for his skilled hand. Sarah, having healed emotionally and internally, was looking forward to the birth of another child. "Maybe it was G-d's will!" she kept saying to herself, wiping a tear from her eye. At the news that she was expecting, Naomi was ecstatic. Her children ran errands for "Aunt" Sarah, only too happy to help. They vaguely remembered the tragedy of losing Chayele but the small graveyard kept that memory alive. It was around that plot that the Jewish community grew. A synagogue was out of the question at this time but religious services were held in one of the larger homes. The women enjoyed getting together to talk and share gossip, as women do. "Women's things."

Sarah seemed to bloom. She was radiant in her pregnancy. She carried well. Soon her time would come. Now there were several women to act as midwives, who knew how to avoid Chayala's problem, who knew how to care for a mother and a baby. One of the newcomers to the town was a "doctor." Well, sort of a doctor, because the law of the land prohibited a Jew from learning medicine in any formal sense. However, when help was needed, the setting of a broken bone, curing a bee sting, rashes, cupping, purging or enemas, he was the "doctor." He had a collection of all kinds of herbs and salves, cures of all sorts on his shelves. If the Christian doctors relied on "bleeding" and expelling "humors" and the church exorcised devils and curses, Meyer, the doctor, used his primitive knowledge and common sense to heal the sick. In short order he was ministering to the neighboring peasants as well as the Jews.

When Sarah was ready, Meyer turned his home over to the women and it became a maternity clinic. Not that it was easy.

At least the men and children were not in the way. This time the baby came naturally, without complications. "Pool Poo!" all the women spat to the side. Seldom had they seen a baby with such white hair and blue eyes or heard such a lusty voice. One of the women whispered, "The tailor has a cantor for a son!" All the women laughed and Sarah laughed, too. "Oy! It hurts to laugh!" she said, smiling down at her little boy. "Go tell Shlomo!" she ordered. "He'll have to get the Moyel from the city." And as she ordered, so arrangements were made for the following week. Eight days later, little Chaim was inducted into the "House of Abraham," the nation of Israel, with cakes and food and wine from the special collection of Nathan's vintage.

The little boy thrived with a lusty appetite for life and for the breast. Chaim, the name means life. As soon as Sarah had realized that she was pregnant, she decided that if it was a boy his name would be Chaim, for the life that Chayele was not able to have. Unknown to them, another baby was born on the day of the bris. The Baron's wife was a frail woman but her beauty masked her weakness. She had raven black hair that made her ivory complexion glow with an incandescent light. It was her eyes, with the depth of night that enchanted the Baron. She was never seen by the people of Watermill but rumor had it that she had the grace and fierceness of the crows that were perched around the Shloss. Great plans were made during her pregnancy. The Baron was elated at the prospect that his beautiful lady was going to bring an heir into the world. He arranged for a doctor from Pilski to attend her. He ordered food and drink for a grand feast on the great day when his son would be born. All the preparations were being carried out, just as the Baroness ordered. He sent a servant to the now-famous tailor of Watermill to fashion a blue and gold robe for the baby. Everything was in readiness. The joyful time had come. The baby however was not a son. It was the most adorable baby girl, so fair and round with raven black hair and eyes as deep as night, forecasting a striking beauty, beyond compare.

The Baroness held her tiny infant lovingly in her arms before the wet nurse took her away. Her wan smile belied her condition as she kissed the tiny forehead and whispered, "Dear Maryushka that will be your name!" As soon as the baby left she closed her eyes as though in sleep and never opened them again. The Baron couldn't believe it. All the joy that his baby had brought was lost in that moment. He was so distraught that he couldn't even speak to order the cancellation of the feast. What a strange irony it was that the whole territory reveled in a frenzy of joy in honor of the birth, while he, the Baron, sat dazed and grieving over his wife's bier. In the tradition of the Baron's family, his privacy was not violated. Even the local priest did not know.

When the doctor returned to Pilski, he arranged for the bishop to return incognito. Alone with his loyal servants, the Baroness was given a Requiem Mass and laid to rest in the crypt behind the small chapel in the bowels of the Shloss. In his grief, the Baron could take no joy in the beautiful cherub his wife had given him. He did not blame the baby. Yet, his broken heart could not understand the injustice of his loss. The wet nurse and the attendants took over the care of Maryushka, who was baptized and christened by the Bishop, right after her mother's interment. It didn't matter that all her dresses were blue and gold; the Baron never saw them, never visited her in her room.

Chaim had the good fortune of not only a loving mother and father to care for him, but a community that treated him like a messiah. The holy books that the Rabbi of Pilski sent regularly for his prize pupil were his riches. Shlomo and Sarah glowed with pride, "Poo! Pool" Not only had Chaim grown into a fine young man, tall, handsome, with cloud-white hair and sky-blue eyes but he had a personality that gave people a warm glow just to be near him. His ready smile and cheerful wit did not hide the brilliant mind that he possessed. He was quick to listen and learn. His father's business thrived, not only because he was a brilliant tailor and an honest man but because of his son's disposition when he tended the customers or delivered their orders. It was over three years since his Bar Mitzvah and the town was still talking about the party that Shlomo and Sarah had made. The tavern wasn't big enough even though Nathan had enlarged it many years before, so that tables and chairs were set with food and wine in the garden behind the tavern. Nathan had built the patio for his customers, when the weather was too hot for drinking indoors. Were it not for the white picket fence the crowd might have trampled Chayele's grave. Shlomo remembered that Sarah, with tears in her eyes, noticing how the guests had encircled the small plot, said, "See Shloymele, our Chayele is celebrating with us too!" She also had reason for tears of joy. For some unknown reason, G-d decided not to allow Sarah to conceive again, after Chaim was born. So she and Shlomo concentrated all their love and attention on the "messiah!"

Watermill had grown quite a bit since the evening of their arrival. But some things had not. The old Bishop of Plilski had died and another anti-Semite had replaced him. The Poles and Jews of Watermill got along reasonably well, but there were signs of hatred showing up. The small church had been replaced by a stone edifice on a hill in the Christian part of town. A young priest, a student of the new bishop, officiated. His sermons, to say the least, were unkind to the Jews. Although serfdom had been all but abolished, the peasantry it seemed were virtual slaves. The Baron was never seen since the Baroness died. He had become a recluse and rumors spread that he had become a monk, had let his hair grow wild and lived on gruel and water. No one really knew but that didn't stop the talk. His commerce and communications with the town continued through his servants. The rent for the land that the Jews built on was collected every month, like clockwork. The horsemen, who were once the Baron's knights, now wore the uniform of the Polish army. Now, as military men they rounded up the young men, the Poles and the Jews alike, for military service. Only a large contribution from Shlomo to their coffers kept them at bay. How they coveted the fair haired boy, the son of the tailor whom they had tried to run off the road many years ago. Every time they came to Shlomo's shop for repairs or to have a uniform made, he would never charge them.

Each time the uniforms would become more elegant than the time before. In spite of their words of appreciation and smiles, deep in Shlomo's heart was the feeling of fear that he felt, that evening when he and his Sarah was heavy with child, ran to the side of the road to avoid being run down. He never forgot that copper kopek, either. In the Shloss, that gray, gloomy structure that stood as a cold monument to the long dead Baroness, a beautiful flower blossomed. Maryushka should have grown up a sad, lonely child, imprisoned by her eccentric father. After all, the only time that she would see him was on religious holidays when the Bishop of Pilski would come to say a private mass for them. Otherwise, her companions were the servants who came to love her as their own. She was taught all the courtesies of the court in preparation for her presentation. She was well trained, courteous and witty. At sixteen, she was shapely and tall, with her sheen raven black hair hanging in a long braid down to her calves and her long eyelashes, arched around her almond-shaped eyes, as dark as night. Since she was born, her clothing was designed by Shlomo, the tailor of Watermill. His expertise and skill had no peer among the many tailors that now set up shop in the town. Whenever Shlomo would go up to the castle with material for her garments, heavy for winter, light for summer, little Chaim would tag along. In time, Chaim would learn how to measure, to fit, to pin and to hem. While his father was busy dealing with the servants, the two children would exchange in pleasantries. He would never forget that she was a Baroness, nobility, a Christian no less, and he, the son of a Jewish tailor. Sarah, in fact, all the Jews saw Chaim as a future Rabbi. He was a brilliant scholar and even though he had learned the tailor's trade, they knew that someday he would be ordained. Chaim thrived on this confidence. He would not disappoint them.

Shlomo's custom had become so overwhelming that he took on several apprentices to help with the work. His ability to demonstrate the work allowed him to avoid speaking, stuttering. Sarah, who had seldom worked in the shop, had to pitch in, too. So when Chaim reached his majority of thirteen years, there was no question that he would be asked to make the trip to the Shloss, with the material, the pins, and the measuring tape to prepare Maryushka's wardrobe. Although they pretended not to be concerned that Chaim took so long, they were. With his ready smile and sparkling eyes he would allay their suspicion with some story. In truth, he couldn't wait for his father to send him back. A crazy, aching feeling took hold in his chest. As he leaned over the Holy Talmud, which he was mastering so easily, he would see the face of Maryushka, her smile, the sheen of her raven black hair. He would hear her chime like laughter as she tried to learn the crazy sounds of his Yiddish expressions. He would shake his head violently but still the image persisted. "Stop it!" his tormented mind kept saying as he forced himself to concentrate on the holy words. And Maryushka would walk around her rooms for days after his visit, lost in her own reverie. His voice kept repeating the funny stories that he always had to tell, the sweet compliments he found to dispel her fears of inadequacy. When he worked around her, she felt like a little dove in the hands of a gentle keeper. Only the governess' tapping cane could bring her back to her lessons in the catechism. But that didn't stop the funny feeling in her breast.

Her sixteenth birthday was soon to come and a small party was being arranged. The governess had taught her all the amenities for the occasion, the role of mistress of the castle. It was to be a special day she was told. She would be presented to her future in-laws and their son, some prince from far away. She had heard all about the nobility but of betrothal and marriage she knew nothing. Even though she seldom heard from her father, it was a shock to hear that he was arranging to get rid of her to some stranger, some prince. That strange feeling she had for Chaim changed into pangs so strong that she could hardly breathe. Chaim was due for the final fitting of her party gown that afternoon. To whom could she confide but him? She couldn't wait for his arrival.

As soon as he arrived, she arranged to send the maids and governess on some errands that would keep them busy for some time. No sooner had he set his things down than she flung herself into his arms, her whole body convulsing in tears. "Oh! Chaim! What am I going to do?" He was so startled that his arms hung at his side. Her grasp was so tight that he could feel her heart through his chest. Involuntarily he reached his arms around her frail bird-like body. She repeated it over and over, "What am I going to do?" Did she hear what he was saying? Did she hear his words?" "I love you, Maryushka! I love you!" And before he knew what was happening, he was kissing the tears on her cheeks, the tears on her lips and in her eyes. Maryushka's tears began to change from tears of sadness to tears of . . . "What are we going to do?" One of the servants returned unexpectedly to find the two embracing. She nearly fainted at the sight. She crossed herself several times, repeating, "Jesus, Mary and Joseph!" Shortly the others returned but by then the lovers had separated. Chaim took up his material and Maryushka dabbed her eyes and affected a smile. The witness said nothing, being the loyal servant who would protect her charge no matter what. Throughout the fitting, Mayushka kept thinking, "What am I going to do?" Chaim was so involved in his own thought of, "What are we going to do?" that he accidentally stuck her with a pin, something he had never done in all the years he had been coming to the Shloss. Before he left, he whispered to her, "G-d will help us, my little angel!" As he departed he saw the witness-servant cross herself again, whispering her invocation to Jesus, Mary and Joseph. Maryushka had to clench her fist to keep from crying. She had to face up to her father. She would never agree to this planned marriage as long as she lived. She couldn't understand why the Lord Jesus had done this cruel thing to her. Her heart belonged to a Jew, a tailor's son, and a rabbinical student, to the bargain. Now she knew what, "Oy! Vey!" meant, one of the phrases Chaim taught her. The thought of her father brought on a fit of rage, a frightening feeling.

Chaim delivered the finished gown and left without saying a word, nor could he if he wanted to. Obviously the witness-servant had confided to the others what she had seen and they stood guard as sentries around a condemned man. No one knew what the girl was going to do. The festive dinner was prepared and the royal guests, although few in number, arrived. The Baron appeared, not as a monk with a cassock and beard but in an elegant robe, the one that he had worn to his own wedding many years before. His shaved face was radiant in spite of the deep shadows around his eyes. He greeted his guests warmly, inviting them to enjoy his hospitality. The servants passed the food and drink to the cheerful toasts of the guests. The moment arrived for the bride-to-be to make her entrance. The big oak door leading to the dining hall slowly opened. Everyone had heard of the beautiful young baroness with the lustrous skin, the raven black braid down to her calves and eyes as dark as night. The Baron had invested quite a sum in the special gown that she was expected to wear. A shock of silence filled the room as Maryushka moved between the open doors. She had found a long black gown that belonged to her mother, no frills, no jewels, no decoration. She had cut her braid and bound her hair tightly over her ears, pinned in the back. Her eyes, red from nights of crying, looked demon like behind her dark eyebrows. It was so strange a sight that everyone felt that they were looking at a huge crow. Before anyone could move or say anything a cawing sound came from her drawn lips. "I will not be the bride of your prince! Even if I have to die!" Abruptly, she turned leaving the huge oak doorway gaping around her receding figure. No one could move or say anything. The Baron, needless to say, was speechless, mortified. The guests slowly set their drinks down, moved away from the table and silently departed. Not since the Baroness, his wife, died had he felt so grieved. "Oh! My G-d," he thought. "Why hadn't the baby died with her mother?" He obviously had no idea why his daughter had done this terrible thing. Had he not given her everything she could need? How had he sinned? "Dear G-d," he thought, "what have I done to deserve this?" There was no answer, only dead silence. If she would defy him, so be it. She had said, ". . . even if I have to die!" So be it! He held the cross that hung from his neck and swore an oath, though he might regret it for the rest of his life. "May I never set eyes on my daughter again! So be it!" The words kept burning into his brain. "So be it!"

Maryushka didn't realize that she had sentenced herself to death. The baron was not a vile man. She would not die a violent death, for he was a Christian nobleman. He gave the order that after the Sunday confession and Mass, the servants would seal the large oak doors to his only daughter's apartment, Maryushka's rooms. No one would attend her with food or company until the day the doors were sealed, for she must fast and pray for her soul, after which the doors would be shut until the coming of Christ. That was his order. So be it!

One whole week would pass until the edict would be carried out. Seven days. The servants were crazy with grief. They kissed her and took care of her needs in spite of the orders. She decided to die, herself, not even knowing about the edict that her father had given. If she couldn't have Chaim, life wasn't worth living. She prayed no more, and read no more from the catechism. In a fit of grief she tore the rosary from her neck and scattered the beads across the wooden floor. She lay down where they had fallen, shattered, as she was, moaning, "My G-d, wherefore hast thou forsaken me?" She had never read those words, yet she spoke them as if they were written on her heart. The governess who loved her as her own, took her up in her arms and led her to bed. "Maryushka, my baby. Tell me what I can do. Tell me anything!" "Anything?" the mournful sound slid from the girl's clenched lips. "All I want, I can't have! All I want is Chaim! He is my heart, my life! Without him there is nothing! Nothing!"

The governess rocked her in her arms when the idea came to her. "What if we send a secret message to Chaim? Maybe he might think of something." Hearing this, Maryushka lifted her head, a small glint of light lit her eyes for a second. What did the governess have in mind? She didn't know, but that didn't stop her. A short message was written detailing all the events that had transpired since he was there in the Shloss. She arranged for him to sneak into the castle and into Maruushka's rooms. The next morning the message was delivered to Shlomo's house by Peterovitch, one of the baron's rent collectors. Chaim took the message and walked out to the small grave site where he used to go to be alone and find solace in times of stress. He read the note carefully, several times, unable to accept the terrible consequences it foretold. He asked Peterovitch to return to him before returning to the Shloss that evening. His heart had never felt so heavy. His head spun with an agony he'd never known. He took his father's credit book and tore a page from the back. Slowly, painstakingly he printed his message. He printed it so it would not be mistaken.

"Sunday evening will begin the holy fast day of Tisha B'Av, the ninth day of Av, when all the Jewish shops are closed and memorial candles are lighted for the mourning of our Temple's destruction. If the door for my coming is open, have the governess place a candle in the window and I will be there. My love cannot die alone!" The governess read the message to Maryushka. All she could say, was, "He will come! He will come!" The silence, the waiting, the numbness weighed heavily upon her but she had no doubt that he would come. The servants prepared for the arrival of the bishop. She confessed and received absolution, in her room. The Baron refused to leave his part of the castle, determined to keep his solemn vow. Even the bishop could not dissuade him. The order was irrevocable. The oak doors would be sealed before the day was over. If the baron never knew that Chaim was involved in this whole situation, how was he to know that there was a conspiracy for Chaim to join Maryushka on that fateful day? The governess had bribed the workmen to delay the sealing of the doors until the twelfth hour, still within the baron's orders.

As soon as it was possible to leave, Chaim was on his way. All he took was his book of psalms. He ran, he stumbled but kept on until he saw in the dark, the flickering light, high up in the window of the Shloss. He cautiously entered the gate, which had been purposely left unguarded, and headed for the unlocked entrance. Silently he leapt up the cold stone steps which he had so often climbed to her rooms, laden with the material and the tools of his trade. He gasped for air, refusing to slacken his pace. He could not wait to have his beautiful Maryushka again in his arms. He had never been in the castle at night, so when he reached her door, the candle light obscured how gaunt and sickly the young lady really looked. As she ran to embrace him, she whispered, "Oh my love! Oh my love! I knew you would come!" His kisses smothered her words. He had come, she thought. G-d had answered her prayers. Alone the two lovers stood embracing as the sound of the workmen began, sealing the great oak doors and their doom. The light in the window, their memorial candle, still flickered in the dark night. The baron refused to leave his room. His doors were sealed, not by workmen with cement, but by grief. Indeed the rumor that he had become a recluse, a monk, now became true. No one except his faithful servants could ever enter his rooms. His diet became gruel and water and his will to live gradually declined. When it came, the whole town mourned his death. Christians. and Jews alike. He had been judicious in keeping the anti-Semitic brutes under control. He had kept Watermill safe, from his office in the Shloss. Now, what would happen? No one knew.

No one, however, understood what happened to Chaim. He had last been seen sitting on the overturned bench in the synagogue, chanting, "The Lamentations." Where he had disappeared to, no one knew. All his things were where he left them, all except the "book of psalms." The candles in Maryushka's room slowly burned down, some beginning to flicker.

The waning light was hardly enough to read by. Chaim didn't need the light to read the psalms, especially the twenty-third. How often had he read it over the grave of the little sister he never knew. Slowly, he began. "A song of David. The Lord is my shepherd, I shall not want. He maketh me to lie down in green pastures. He leadeth me beside the still waters." He paused between each line to translate the Hebrew words to Maryushka. She never heard such beautiful poetry before. The images seemed to raise her spirits. His loving voice enveloped her with a warmth only his arms had done before.

"Ssss!" A strange sound seemed to issue from the dark alcove in the corner of the room. "Ssss!" again. Chaim closed the book. Was the candle playing tricks on him or was something moving toward them? It was too soon for the Angel of Death to claim them. Hardly discernible was the governess, who stood before them. She had secreted herself in the alcove unknown to anyone. She could not bear to leave her beloved baby, even when she was condemned to die behind those sealed doors. She had been her mother's governess, when she was a child, something Maryushka had never known all these years. She had been a devoted servant to the dear departed baroness, and at her bedside she swore to care for the baby girl as if it were her own. As a child, her mother, the baroness, had accidentally discovered a secret passageway which only she and the governess knew about. It was a crazy labyrinth that connected these rooms to a hidden slab far outside the gate. The secret passageway was never used by Maryushka's mother because any sound in the tunnel could be heard throughout the castle. The governess had put together a bundle of clothes and some food that would be needed to successfully escape from the edict. The baron's confidence that Maryushka was entombed in the Shloss must never be broken.

The three fugitives traveled as fast as they could, as fast as the weakened Maryushka could. Their escape must never be suspected. With the help of many Jewish communities, they were able to get food and shelter on their long journey eastward to the Russian border. Having the training as a tailor would help them settle anywhere, once they felt they would be safe. Along the way, the governess decided to stay at a Russian Orthodox convent where she could rest her weary body and wait for G-d to take her. There were plenty of parting tears as the young couple continued on their journey. That Maryushka had the strength to travel under such difficult conditions was just another miracle among so many. Finally, they decided to stop. It was a fair-sized city that boasted a large Jewish community, a synagogue, a school for Jewish children and even a Yeshiva. No one suspected that Maryushka wasn't Jewish. All along the long trek to this haven he had been teaching her Yiddish. She loved him for his patience and anything he said, she learned. The Polish that they spoke was not that unusual, although slightly different from the Russian dialect spoken in this new city. Knowledge of the universal Yiddish language made them welcome throughout the pale.

After getting settled on the "Shneider Gass," the tailor's street, Chaim arranged for a conference with the chief rabbi. He told the rabbi, in strict confidence, the whole story and of their flight. The rabbi listened intently. After some time elapsed since Chaim finished, the old man stroked his beard several times, as was his habit, and spoke slowly, deliberately. "Listen, my child. First, that you love this woman, is obvious. That she loves you, after all that you've been through, is also obvious. But aside from everything, you can't live with this woman!" Chaim interrupted, "Rabbi, we've never been intimate!" The rabbi merely said, "Mm! In any case, she is an outsider, a Christian. You know the law. Has she ever made known any intention to accept the burden, our faith?" Chaim sat there mute, dumbfounded. The subject never came up. With all his learning, Chaim realized how foolish he was. It had never come up because he had never thought about it. All his mind and body were devoted to, was survival. Now he realized how negligent he had been toward his duty as a devout Jew. But he never said anything about that now. Let the rabbi talk, he thought, and so he did. "The Almighty, praised be He, has led you from the jaws of death to this fair city, you and the lady. Go in peace! When it is convenient for her, have her come to see me. Do not coax her. Say nothing to her about our talk. Our loving G-d will resolve this problem!" Chaim returned home and gave the message to Maryushka, just as the rabbi said.

After a year of intense study and guidance from the rabbi and his wife, Maryushka was received into the House of Israel and her name was changed to Miriam. The rabbi pointed out that it was the name of Moses' sister, who had saved him from death, from an edict of the Pharoah, just as she was saved from death and the baron's edict. Shortly after, it was announced that on the Lag B'Omer holiday, Chaim and Miriam would be married. Secretly, by special courier, Chaim sent a letter to Watermill, to Shlomo, the tailer. The invitation to the wedding was simple, no explanation, no story. The message was clear enough, their son Chaim was safe. He read the invitation over and over to Sarah and each time they wept. No greater joy could they have. Shlomo and Sarah had never accepted the notion that their son had met with a fatality. Now their faith was rewarded as they stood under the wedding canopy with their handsome blond, blue-eyed son. Sarah adored the raven-haired beauty who stood beside him. Shlomo couldn't believe that his Chaim and the baby baroness were here, together. The rabbi began to chant, "How beautiful are thy tents, oh, Jacob . . ." but Chaim and Miriam did not see the tents. They saw the Shloss, the gray, cold castle at the edge of Watermill, so many miles away. This had to be Shlomo and Sarah's secret. Even in their joy, they still would have to protect the children from the baron's edict. No one must ever know that Maryushka had escaped, escaped with Chaim to this new life.

If you were told what happened next, you wouldn't believe it. Chaim and Miriam were soon blessed with a beautiful, healthy baby girl. When Shlomo and Sarah received the news they took a bouquet of daises out to the small grave behind the tavern and prayed. "Dear G-d! Let this new Chayele have a long and happy life!" And so she did, along with her many brothers and sisters. Chaim prospered in his profession as a tailor and his shop was to become renowned not only as a place of learning the trade but as a yeshiva for learning Torah. Miriam became known as the Rebbitzin around whom the women of the city gathered with love and respect. As for Shlomo and Sarah, they basked in the joy that the letters brought them. For all the happy occasions they would arrange a convenient reason to travel to the big city in Russia and they were lucky that there were no sad ones. They noticed that Chaim had begun using the family name, Slomovitch, something that the government now required. The secret of the past was never revealed to anyone outside the immediate family and in time that too was forgotten. Only the fact that the family had come from the town of Watermill in Poland, many years ago, was remembered.

Strange as it may seem, in Watermill, no one really knew why the pilgrimage to the Shloss was made every year on Lag B'Omer, the holiday of spring and weddings. Some mysterious power seemed to urge the children to go up the path and through the old rusty gates of the Shloss. Something strange always seemed to urge some boy, this time Benny, another time Moishe, and someone else in the future, to throw a rock at the old oak doors and scatter the crows from their nests. And among those crows, flying out from the Shloss, everyone believed, were the spirits of the baron, the baroness his wife, and Chaim, the tailor's son who had disappeared and his beloved Maryushka, the beautiful young baroness with hair like the raven and eyes as dark as night.

Epilogue

TIME HAS THE power of making amends for terrible beginnings. Watermill past soon faded in the memory, and the subsequent generations became disinterested in what seemed to be more fiction than fact. So the Slomovitch family lost any connection with the shtetl called Watermill, so far away in Poland, almost.

EM

The Watermill Story

II

Preface

THE PEACEFUL, IDYLLIC setting of Watermill hadn't changed but the climate of fear had. Many of the Jews emigrated to other parts of the world. Still others chose to remain, bound by loyalty, the past, religious fervor. That the German invasion was imminent was clear to the young, not dangerous to the elderly, the infirm or their guardians, who became the first victims of the assault in Poland and Watermill before the "Holocaust!"

EM

Acknowledgement: For interest, encouragement and friendship: Frances Taormina, Bette Cyzner, Teri McMann, Helen Karpp, Dr. Martin H. Levinson, Theresa Riccardi of UFT Creative Writing Class.

The Watermill Story

I

1939, SEPTEMBER 28TH, Von Ribbentrop and Molotov had signed their non-aggression pact. The German troops had crossed into Poland and were more than half way across the land where the Blitzkrieg had taken them, when they were pushed back by the Red Army. Not soon enough for the Jews and Poles who were killed by the bloodthirsty Nazi beasts. The town of Watermill was one of the many towns and cities that lay just within the territory that they had initially conquered. The Russians were able to push the Germans out of the area for a short time until the pact returned it to the Germans. The Oder-Niesse line agreed to in the Russo-German non-aggression pact put Watermill back in the grip of the German death trap, again. For the lucky ones, the massed German army on the Polish border, that summer, was enough of a warning. Many fled eastward, to the uncertainty, the dangers of Russia. Considering the odds of survival if they were to stay, many Jews, not enough, gathered whatever they could carry and kissed their families goodbye, surely forever, and fled, some to the Red Army, some to the underground and some to Siberian camps. Now that the Deutscher Panzer Division had occupied the town again, the Commandant decided that the old castle, the Shloss at the edge of town, would be the perfect headquarters for his central command. It would take quite a bit of work to restore the condition of the huge oak doors and the interior, as it had been unoccupied for decades, except for the ghosts, rumor said. All the stories the Mayor had told him about the Shloss made it more intriguing. Now, sitting on the Mayor's desk, smoking a Royal Cuban cigar, the general gave orders for a brigade of Polish men and women to convert the haunted relic into a comfortable Division Headquarters.

The Mayor would retain all civil authority as long as it did not conflict with the German military plans. The castle would be perfect. If there was talk of ghosts, of a baron, a baroness and a daughter, well he didn't believe in ghosts inside the castle or out. The general had resolved the major problem when his troops were in Watermill before. "Judenrein!" He had taken care of all the Jews then. All were gone! All that was in the Juden section of town had been rounded up. He remembered how pleased he was to see how compliant they were, how they had dug the trench out behind the tavern, on the little hill where a small grave stood. With a smile on his ordinarily grim face, Reich General Neimueller thought about how it looked as the Shmeisser submachine guns picked them off and how they seemed to disappear as their lifeless bodies fell into the ditch. He recalled how the Polish townsfolk stood silently by as though they enjoyed the sport. These Poles, he knew, would make perfect slaves and he was proven correct. As soon as the last body disappeared, they eagerly went to work covering the ditch, erasing the scene of the massacre, erasing the Jews, the killers of their G-d.

No sooner had the mayor gotten the order to get the castle prepared than he commandeered the men and women to do the work. The troops had moved in and began to search all of the homes for any communists or Jews that may have returned since the retreat. It was both disappointing and gratifying that none were found. The troops were ordered to the railroad yards for bivouac. The salt mines outside of Watermill had become a lucrative source of income for the once small town, so the railroad company had built a large depot for shipping of the raw material. This was a bonus for the capture of Watermill. Therefore it was spared the violent destruction that the armies of Germany and the U.S.S.R. had visited on other Polish towns. The Reich could use this important commodity and under military control the mining would certainly be made much more efficient, a twenty-four-hour-a-day operation. There were plenty of strong Polish bodies to utilize.

The records that were confiscated from the Town Hall were still intact and would help officers carry out their mission. One thing he had decided about the "Shloss" was that under no circumstances would the "Gestapo Dogs" be allowed to use it for their base. Let them occupy the old courthouse, the Magistrat. He despised the "Black and Skull" S.S. men who tried to derail his career by accusing him of Jew ancestry. He, Heinrich Neimueller, was a proud and pure Arian. His family fought against the Reformation and the Huns before that. His allegiance was to Germany. If Hitler and the Nazis were the vehicle for Germany's victory over the decadent world, all the better. He did not believe in brutality, like the Gestapo. Only killing. After all a soldier's job was to carry out his orders, to kill.

Within a week, the castle shined. One could see what a magnificent edifice the baron had originally built. What a waste it would be to have it remain abandoned after all those years, because of some silly superstition. In the military sense, it was now "spit and polish!" The furnishings were confiscated from the "Magistrate" before the Gestapo could stop him. The old ivy was stripped from the front walls of the castle and huge swastika flags were draped over them. New generators were installed to insure constant lighting and electricity because there was always the possibility of sabotage to the Polish electrical supply. Renovations to modernize it were also made for it to become the general's command post.

As Herr General Neimueller, with a hard "G," walked around his new home, a sense of pride swelled in his heart. Hitler, Der Feuhrer, lived in a hole in the ground, while he, a lowly soldier, had this immense castle. "What an irony," he crowed, "Jew ancestry, hell!" The only other change to the Shloss that one could see was the forest of antennas that rose from the high turrets where once brave knights stood watch over the baron's domain. This was modern warfare and electronic communications was the most important element in the successful movement of troops.

A sharp knock came from the huge oak door of his office. This was the baron's room; with the tapestry cleaned and refurbished and modern lighting replacing the torch light of centuries before, the room was now quite handsome and comfortable. "Things are going quite well!" he thought aloud, dragging on his delicious cigar. "Komen!" he ordered. The room already reeked of his cigar smoke and a cloud of Havana's best hung in the air. A lieutenant entered the room and snapped to attention, his arm outstretched in the Nazi salute. "Heil Hitler!" Neimueller waved a sloppy "Heil!" back at him. "Herr General (with a hard 'G'). There has been an accident at the mine!" Lieutenant Holtz shouted.

The general calmly interrupted. "Just get some more Polacks to replace the dead ones! That's not too hard!"

"B-but mein Herr!" the Lieutenant stuttered. "It wasn't the peasants. It was our soldiers, who were on guard duty!" The officer paused to catch his breath. "A tragedy. The Poles reported that only the soldiers were killed. Something happened to the lighting and there was a strange noise and when the lights went on the guards were all lying face down in the brine!"

Now the general began to shout questions. "Were there any signs of sabotage? Was there blood on the bodies? Weren't you supposed to be in charge, man?"

The lieutenant meekly answered, "The Poles were being escorted out after their shift. We found all the guards but one and they were removed to the bivouac hospital. I ordered an autopsy from the doctor. He said it would take days." The general's eyes were fierce with anger, almost disbelief that such a strange "accident" could happen under his command. He seemed to calm down, but his brain told him that the Gestapo would have a field day with this catastrophe.

"And the men have been replaced?" he quietly asked, controlling his temper.

"Immediately, sir!" the lieutenant snapped.

"Let me know the doctor's report as soon as it is ready! Meanwhile, have Miklovitch, the Polish foreman snoop around for leads. It smells like rotten herring, the kind we got in Old Amsterdam!" he concluded. With a sloppy salute and a "Heil" he dismissed the lieutenant, who was beginning to get dizzy from the cigar stench. The general relit the cigar stub as he thought, "Something very fishy, indeed!" The huge oak door closed behind the officer as he left the room. The next day, the six-foot naked cadaver of the missing soldier was found under the dirty work clothes in the back of the dark locker room. Like the death of the other soldiers, this too was a mystery. All of the Polish slaves, forced to work in the mines regardless of what their real life jobs had been, had no idea what happened when the lights went out. Everyone thought that reprisals would come and they were afraid that they would suffer some punishment, even death, but none came. After all, they were told that the general was not a brutal man,

Several days passed and the doctor's report was delivered by an orderly. The general read and reread the paper. Some of the terminology was difficult but the strangest part was that there was absolutely no sign of foul play, sabotage or murder. None! Not even a heart attack! Just dead! The doctor had tested for food poisoning; every known forensic examination available was made. "Nein! Nothing!" The general thought, "If these men died from nothing, whom can I blame? No one!" He signed the death certificates, "Killed honorably in the line of duty!" and arranged for the bodies to be sent to their respective homes. He waited for the Gestapo to bother him but nothing happened. He was relieved! He turned to his map and mused about getting his staff together for a strategy session. Berlin expected a major push and he was in the middle of it. The smoke from his Havana wafted across the map like clouds of the blitzkrieg he was planning.

The town of Watermill sat in a valley, on the edge of the Carpathian Mountains; its setting was idyllic. From his window in the Shloss, the one from which the baron had loved to look over his domain, the general was able to see all the way to the mountain tops, even without his Zeiss-Ikon binoculars. However, he occasionally would pick them up to watch the convoys wend their way up the twisting roads. "Someday," he thought, "we'll build good roads like the fantastic Autobahn instead of these dirty mule paths!"

Rrrrrrring! Rrrrrrring! He reached for the phone. The high-pitched sound always jarred his nerves. How he would have preferred the Bzzzzzz! of a field telephone. He picked up the receiver. "Ja! Heil!" he shouted into it, not trusting those frail things made of brass, confiscated from some French Jew's factory outside of Paris. A voice from message center, a floor below, was babbling through the damned French telephone, "something . . . . motorized unit . . . . detachment . . . . scouting mission . . . ." "Halt!" he shouted into the phone. He then realized that he had been holding it upside down. Cursing under his breath, "those damned French . . . ." he corrected the position of the receiver and shouted into the mouthpiece,

"Who the Hell is this?" The timid voice at the other end identified himself, his name, and rank. Slowly, he repeated the whole message that he had rushed through before.

"A whole motorized unit, a detachment under his orders, on a scouting mission looking for guerrillas, had driven into a ravine somewhere in the mountains. Coordinates to follow. One of the few survivors, although severely hurt, had finally been able to phone in. Herr Kapitan von Ratten had followed the road sign direction. No one expected that they were running off a cliff one hundred meters high!" There was no reply when the soldier finished.

The general gasped in disbelief. This wasn't even a military action where one could expect losses due to stupidity. This wasn't even an ambush set up by the Underground. He was losing more men here, around Watermill, than he was at the front. In disbelief, he shouted into the phone, "Didn't the idiot use a scout car?" After all, it was simply expected military procedure, especially in occupied enemy territory. What about a road map? Simple precaution! How could the captain be so stupid or naive as to trust a sign, a Polish sign, that anyone could have planted?

The voice at the other end of the line answered, "I don't know, Mein Herr General! I'm only the message center." The general, now a little calmer, told the soldier to get his adjutant on the phone and get him to organize a rescue party as soon as the exact coordinates were received. "It was all those Nazi officers at headquarters who were promoting these green officers without any of the necessary training!" he concluded. Either his men were very stupid or the enemy was very smart. No way! Not smarter than Reich's General Neimueller. No way!" He had the record and the medals to show for it. He knew that there would be sporadic efforts by the local enemy to do harm to the war effort but they were no match to this Reich's General.

II

These instances of Polish Guerrilla action against his men would not be disruptive to his army's movement toward the east. The Feuhrer's strategy was understood very well and the operation was moving according to plan. Little opposition was being encountered except for these local deaths, well, murders. Actually, they were becoming more frequent and harder to explain to HQ. He must do something soon because the troops in Watermill were becoming demoralized. He certainly didn't want the Gestapo dogs coming in and disrupting his command with their brutal tactics. After all, Hitler's staff was very pleased with him and what he was doing on the front as well as in Watermill, except for these accidents.

In addition to the salt mine and the Shloss, the town had become a rear RandR area. The hospital was now equipped to handle more serious wounds, and the houses that had been in the Jew section were converted to brothels. The houses farthest from the Shloss were to be designated for the enlisted men and the better ones that were closer, were only for the officers. Of course the general's staff could have discreet visits to their quarters, although this was officially discouraged. This privilege was greatly abused by the elite officers and the general was able to use it as leverage over his staff. After all, he was of the "Honey and Vinegar" school of discipline. Although most of his staff was married men, who were devoted husbands and fathers, honorable officers of the Third Reich, but like all good jobs, there were fringe benefits. The women received no monetary compensation, which made it legitimate and not prostitution, heaven forbid.

Maryushka was young for a Madame and she kept telling the girls that slavery was bad but death was worse. She had met with the general shortly after the second occupation and the girls were invited to become "hostesses." She had set up a list of rules about abuse, drunkenness and the right of refusal. The rules were posted and the men understood that the girls needed privacy and were "Off-limits" at certain times. The general signed on to these conditions and except for the exceptional brawl or stupidity, things were under control. The old Jew tavern was stocked with kegs of beer from Munich and chits were honored by the Polish bartender who confiscated the place when the Jewish owner was removed, during the first occupation, planted in the garden with the rest of the Jews, behind the tavern, where the single grave used to be.

This Maryushka had the same name but was no relation to the baroness who, it was believed, died in the tower of the Shloss many years ago and was thought to be haunting it to this day. The name was the same but, it was said, looked nothing like her. The baroness, it was told, was thin, with raven black hair and eyes like the night, while this Maryushka was blond as the noonday sun, with sky blue eyes, a pug nose and full, plump breasts. No one looking at her grace and charm would have dreamed that she was a Jew, the only remaining one, to have witnessed the slaughter of her people. Some of her family had fled before the Nazis came the first time but she had a job to do, actually a job that had nothing to do with the brothel.

Watermill had a middle-aged priest at this time. He was a local man who grew up and went to the local Polish school in the parish, with Jewish boys and girls as well as Catholics. When it happened, he was appalled at the massacre but could say nothing for fear of the consequences. His duty was to the Church, his Pope and the Concordat that Pope Pius XII had made with Hitler. He offered the Jews his protection if they would agree to convert to Catholicism. He even offered to arrange "fixed" birth certificates for them to prove their Christian ancestry but no one accepted the offer. Now he received the "ladies" in the confessional and gave them absolution and he buried the Polish victims that the salt mine constantly provided. He even pretended to hear Maryushka's confession, when she reported to him the secret military information which was gleaned from the soldiers in their moments of passion. Only she knew that the good father was the secret conduit for information to the Underground around Watermill.

Only they knew that a large convoy of military material was being shipped, prepared for transfer to the front and that it was going to pass over the Pilski Bridge, twenty miles away. This route had become necessary because the old Watermill Bridge had been washed away in the early spring flash flood. This was a mystery in itself because there had not been any heavy rainstorm or quick ice thaw that might have caused it to happen. The Germans saw it as a catastrophe, the Poles saw it as a miracle. Surely, they knew it was an inconvenience to them both. The general knew that it did impede the war effort a little; however, in truth the old bridge would not have been able to sustain the heavy loads that the trucks were carrying in the convoy.

The secret convoy set out in the dead if night. Special precaution was taken, no lights, no sounds. Even the heavy Volkswagen eight-wheelers had been fitted with special mufflers to hide the action. The Feuhrer had personally called Neimeuller to explain the vital importance of this convoy, which was carrying all the winter supplies as well as the needed ammunition. "Ve must supply all our Panzers for the final push!" Hitler shouted over the private line. "Uncle Cho doesn't stand a chance! Ha! Ha! You got it, Heinz?" There was no reply because the Feuhrer had hung up before one could be given. Talk, the Wehrmacht didn't need. It needed action and action it would get. The convoy moved out on the twenty miles toward Pilski. What ordinarily would take less than one hour to drive, stretched into two, almost three. They had to cross the bridge before dawn or the mission would be compromised.

Absolute radio silence was adhered to and no lights on the vehicles. Each vehicle had phosphorescent paint on it to avoid collisions and the motors were soundproofed. They all moved slowly but steadily, as the world slept around them. Up ahead lay Pilski, a modem city with paved roads, wide enough for large transport. Its silhouette could hardly be seen as it moved silent in the deep dark night. The lead car rolled cautiously across the steel bridge. Safe! The clear signal was given and the massive trucks edged forward. They had taken all the necessary precautions to avoid the kind of tragic accident that happened in the ravine. The lead convoy moved across, nearing the far side. No problem!

Rrrrrrring! Rrrrrrring! The general deep in sleep, jumped up six inches from the bed. Before he landed, his hand grasped the telephone just as the third ring was beginning. "G-d, how I hate that phone!" he thought. "That abrasive ring only brought bad news. Who screwed up this time?" He thought he had the best command support, at least until he set up in this damned place, Watermill. Maybe it was true. Maybe the castle is haunted, after all. Maybe some spirits were working against him. Since he'd been here, all kinds of weird accidents had plagued him. And the Gestapo, he was sure, was plotting against him, with their dossiers full of reports about all the catastrophes that were happening under his command. He held the receiver limply in his hand. The voice at the other end was frantic. His head was still half asleep as his mind became more alerted to the noises at the other end of the line. He looked out of the window. Good! It was not dawn yet.

"Ja! Vas is los!" he was able to hear himself shout into the delicate brass phone that he hated. The voice at the other end stopped abruptly and again began from the beginning, like a phonograph record repeating itself

"Herr General!" (with a hard 'G') the voice began. The voice was not familiar immediately although it was his liaison officer stationed in Pilski. "I can hardly speak," the officer continued, his voice filled with shock, fear, disbelief "We checked every day for the last week. We had sentries posted, twenty-four hours a day. Believe me, it was strong, perfect. The lead car went over and the trucks followed. It couldn't have been the weight. The bridge structure was sound, I swear by my honor as an engineer, an officer and a gentleman!"

"Stop your blubbering!" the general interrupted. "What the hell happened? Was there a bomb, an explosion?"

"Mein General, no sooner than all the main trucks with the arms were on the bridge than it begun to collapse like match sticks. As soon as the first truck hit the river bed it exploded into a ball of flame, igniting the next and the next. Mein Herr, look out your window, you can see the flames, the shells and mortars are flying everywhere! The river is ablaze with petrol and the trucks in the convoy that were on the bridge have been set afire by the exploding arsenal. Our soldiers are dying and the people of Pilski are running for their lives. I was finally able to reach a telephone to call you. Mein Gott! This is terrible!"

The general hung up, not even saying, "Good bye!" He immediately dialed his adjutant and dispatched the lieutenant to Pilski, to assess the situation. "Don't even dress!" he screamed. "I want a full report, yesterday, do you hear, YESTERDAY!"

The report was filed with the general's secretary; copies were filed with the other reports of unsolved murders. A shiver went down her back. If we are the invincible force, than how is it that all these "accidents" keep happening? Was it her imagination, or was the portrait of the Feuhrer behind his desk scowling at her for thinking such traitorous thoughts? Since her typewriter had stopped its chattering, the general sat at his desk reading and rereading the whole report. He kept shaking his head in disbelief. Where was the leak about this "Top Secret" transport? Everyone involved in the operation had been ordered to silence and been sequestered for weeks. It was called quarantine. All the officers were briefed about complete secrecy of the mission. The security around the convoy had been double-checked, triple-checked. Nothing in the report gave the slightest clue as to how this tragic accident could possibly have happened. No sign of sabotage could be found. No indication that someone in his unit was at fault. There was no explosion before the collapse. Perhaps, if he had ordered each truck to advance across the bridge by itself, this might not have happened but that would have been inefficient and the convoy would have been discovered by daylight. The Fuehrer would be furious that the enemy could destroy the great German army even before it left the occupied territories. He would be absolutely right in removing the general from his command. If the Fuehrer ordered that he be shot for his incompetence, he would be absolutely justified. The Gestapo, which he had kept off his back until now, would be negligent in not pursuing him, picking at his bones like the crows that nested in the walls of the Shloss. His troops at the front were doing fine. Here at Watermill everything seemed cursed, cursed by the ghosts that, it was said, haunted the castle and flew around it as crows, an omen of death. How could he think such superstitious nonsense? What was happening to his self-confidence? He was the general! Wasn't he in charge? Well, there was one thing that he could do. He had a buddy in Intelligence, in Berlin. Kolonel von Schmidt had come up through the ranks with him, had been the closest friend in the Military Academy and throughout his career; if anyone could resolve these terrible accidents, he could. He wrote the request; message center encoded it and sent it via radio transmission to the High Command. Why hadn't he thought of this before? Von Schmidt had been a brilliant tactician in the field and had it not been for someone's stupidity in ordinance development, he would have been the one in charge of this command. The colonel had lost the sight of both eyes but not his brilliant mind. Hitler had relied on him until now for intelligence but if the message was clear, Von Schmidt would be on loan to him.

III

Far away in the Russian capital, in the Kremlin, an officer of the Red Army was being briefed in German Intelligence. His credentials were top grade. He was tall, blond, blue-eyed and brilliant. He had been a professor of foreign languages, Polish, Hungarian, German, Czech, in addition to the other major European languages. General Zhukov had requested him for his staff but Marshal Stalin had other ideas. He needed an inside man, someone who could get top secret information about the Wehrmacht's plans; otherwise, the Soviet forces were in big trouble. How to get this accomplished was the problem, until now. The message from the Shloss had been intercepted but it was in code that could not be deciphered. The reply from Berlin, also received, was of no use because it too could not be read. What was so disturbing, was that it was obviously so important that none of the usual systems were used. It was impenetrable. Lieutenant Slomovitch was called in to work out the solution. It took several attempts without any solution; then he tried a German dialect that had not been used for many generations. In fact he had learned it from his grandmother, whose mother had come from a small town in Poland. No one realized that Josef Slomovitch was a Jew. The "J" had been omitted from his I.D. card and his records and he was not raised as a Jew. The tow-headed kid should have fit right in with the other Russkies, but he actually didn't fit in. He was an exceptionally brilliant student who enjoyed studies more than playing, the challenge of education to fun and games. That did not mean that this tall, strong, lean man wasn't an excellent athlete as well. His teachers from the beginning of his education through university looked forward to having him in their classes. If it wasn't for his gregarious personality and generous smile, the other students would have resented him. Even in the army, the career officers had to accept the fact that he was top notch. Now, Josef had solved the secret message. He carefully burned the original message center copy and every scrap associated with it. The solution was in his head and he would share it with no one except the very top generals, Zhukov or Voroshilov. No one else! What would they make of this request to Berlin High Command for the blind colonel? Zhukov gave it his immediate attention. He realized that if the colonel was being asked for, then General Neimeuller must be in deep trouble. The Underground was doing its job in slowing down the Wehrmacht's advance. The action that the guerrillas were taking, although sporadic, was helping. Although the truce and the Pact had allowed some extra time to get the Red Army ready, it wasn't ready enough. In several hours, the lieutenant had a plan. If Stalin approved, it would be set in motion immediately.

IV

The Benz sedan motorcar with its Nazi flags flying from the fenders sped from Pilski, the sight of the great disaster, to Watermill, the command post of General Neimeuller. The car's chauffeur kept describing the scenery to his sightless passenger. The much-decorated colonel was tall in his seat, the German shepherd seeing eye dog panting lightly beside him.

"How much further?" he asked, his impatience beginning to show.

"According to the map, Mein Herr Kolonel," the driver replied, "twenty miles or so." With the peaked cap low on his forehead and dark glasses that he wore, one could hardly tell what a handsome man he was. Although the explosion had affected his sight, it had not caused any disfigurement. His blond, almost white hair, his sightless blue eyes, hidden from view, and boyish appearance masked the very serious contemplation that his relaxed demeanor displayed. The canvas top had been removed and the scent of the hillside blew into his face, getting his custom-made uniform and his decorations to flutter like the swastika banners in the front of him. Although he was eager to arrive, he ordered the driver to take his time. And so it was, the Colonel enjoyed the smell of the grassy knolls and the sounds of the fields, which sighted people seldom notice. "When we will have won this dreadful war, all the world will be peaceful as this." he mused. The driver carefully took the turns in the road so as not to upset his charge and the dog. Neither had noticed that their trip was being marked by the peasants in the fields, to be reported to the Underground later in the day. They could tell that it was an important officer of rank, but nothing more. Soon the car was at the top of a hill where the colonel could feel their descent into the valley.

"Mein Kolonel!" the driver shouted into the wind, "There on the horizon, a castle, a large castle. Not as ornate as the ones that we have on the Rhine but large enough!" Before long he was submitting his credentials to the sentry at the gate of the Shloss, the German word for castle from the time this was the land of the Kaiser. The safety bar that had been erected was raised, and the colonel was driven up the driveway right to the huge wooden doors. As soon as the vehicle came to a stop, the driver set the brake and ran around to open the half-door for the colonel, who had taken the harness of the dog, slid over and alighted from the car to the cobblestone path.

"Well, Fritz!" he said to the dog, "This is our new home!" As he moved forward he could hear the sentry snap to attention, so he faced the sound and curtly gave a reply salute. The huge oak doors were opened and Fritz guided the colonel into the large entryway. An orderly came over, introduced himself and guided the colonel with due military courtesy, to a room where he could freshen up from the long, dusty trip. Several soldiers were dispatched to bring the colonel's luggage in from the motorcar. He had taken one with him, refusing to allow anyone to help him with it. Everything had been prepared to make such an important guest comfortable. Obviously, the general would see to his every need.

A signal was immediately sent up to the general that his friend had arrived, and that he would be available shortly. Neimeuller could hardly contain himself. It had been too long since they had been buddies together, long since the terrible accident to his eyes. Downstairs, the colonel asked the orderly to have Fritz fed and kenneled. With a smart heel-clicking salute, the orderly was dismissed and he left with the dog. With his white walking stick, the colonel stood there as his aid approached to meet him and escort him to the general's quarters. Acoustically this place was wonderful because it made every sound direction easy to read, he thought. No sooner had he stepped into the general's large office when he heard Neimeuller push back his chair on its coasters, rise and call across the room.

"Erich! My dear friend, Erich! How long has it been? Ach! Never mind, too long! I have ordered some dinner, we'll talk, and after you've had a good night's sleep, we'll get to the problem. By the way, let me take your bag!"

In all the excitement and talk, Neimeuller forgot to offer the colonel a seat. "Forgive me!" he blurted out, "Here's a comfortable chair!" as he shoved a lounge chair over for the colonel to sit in. Erich eased himself into the chair and waited for the general to stop to catch his breath. Herr Neimeuller had always been a chatterbox but this was ridiculous. Speaking of breath, the colonel politely asked that the dinner be served somewhere else. He wouldn't come right out and say that the cigar stench made him sick, so he graciously made up some excuse not to dine in the office. The officers' mess hall was cleared and dinner was served in private. The scent of the Sauerbraten preceded it into the dining hall, along with spaetzels and katuffel. The best Moselle wine was poured. A restaurant couldn't have done better. They toasted the Fuehrer, the Wehrmacht, and the Third Reich. There was plenty of small talk about the past, family and friends, the war and nonsense, like the jokes that were going around about Mussolini and Stalin. It had gotten late when the colonel followed the orderly up to his sleeping quarters and his office, the small bag in his hand.

It was hardly light when he was awakened by the screeching crows. "What the hell of a way to be called from sleep!" he thought as he sat up and flung his legs over the side of the immense bed. Of course, he had tested the limits of its size the night before, as he always had in strange surroundings but this morning, he thought, this must be some antique. Beds are not made this way anymore. He was surprised to hear the aide knock on the door, from the sound of which, he surmised, it must have been hewn of large solid oak. A fresh uniform was ready for him, with the appropriate insignia. The plumbing renovations the general had ordered for the Shloss had also included bathing and toilet facilities in all the major rooms, by no means fancy, but adequate. After a quick shower and with some discreet help from the orderly, he appeared fresh and ready for the day ahead. The general met him in the dining hall, where all stood at attention until the general and the colonel took their seats at the Command Table to the side of the great hall. This was a great honor because the general usually dined alone, in his quarters.

Before leaving for their private talk, the colonel requested that Fritz be let out of the kennel so he could run around the compound. It was a beautiful day before, but a cloud of despair seemed to hang over them as the general recounted the tragic accidents which he knew were murders. The colonel listened intently, making mental notes. When the general finished the overall picture, von Schmidt interrupted with a request for a secretary. It was obvious that with all the data and specific information he needed to solve these cases, he would need help. He assumed that a young man would be assigned to him, so when the scent of sweet lilies wafted over him and the delicate step of a young lady approached, he was pleasantly surprised. She stopped a few feet in front of him. She had been instructed of his condition and her duties. She snapped to attention and in a sharp military voice, announced, "Mein Kolonel! Korporal Helga Zeiss to serve you." Immediately, the delicate image of the lilac maiden disappeared, replaced by a stiff iron maid of the Third Reich Youth Corps. In fact, every movement that she made signaled the stiffly starched uniform that kept her erect and at attention even when she was relaxed.

He decided that he would have to be extremely formal, something that he had not planned, considering the scent and the gender of the secretary. She led him to a room with a desk and typewriter where he could dictate his orders. The lilac scent was distracting him, so he requested that she open the window. "What a stinking place," he thought, "either Cuban cigar smoke or lilac perfume to choke me to death. Didn't they realize that the sense of smell was enhanced with the loss of sight?" The fresh air soon dissipated the scent and he began to feel comfortable in the large leather recliner that she had led him to.

"Ready, Korporal?" he began. "Number one! I will need a wire recorder to record messages for your transcription. And plenty of electric wire! Two! The room that I live in now will be changed! There is a room at the top of the Shloss that is unoccupied, because the heavy oak doors were sealed with mortar many years ago. They will be opened. It will be cleared out and made into my private bedroom and office, immediately! Have the antique bed that I slept in last night transferred up to my new quarters. As to bathing and so forth, arrangements will be made! After this is done, we will get down to work! Understood?" Her snappy reply was accepted with a return salute, and her stiff uniform rose and marched out of the room. "If only the scent wasn't so strong," he thought.

The general could not understand the reason for those requests but if Erich had ordered them, he would comply. Being blind and brilliant entitled him to be eccentric. This wasn't the same man that he had known years before, but times change and so do people. He was puzzled by the request for that room. It was the only one in the Shloss which had the most difficult access, a single winding stone stairway which would be hard to negotiate even by a sighted person. Apparently, the colonel did not believe in ghosts. Why had he also insisted that a double bolt be installed on both sides of the door, was a puzzle, too. Neimeuller decided that if the colonel could solve the mysterious accidents, then any weird requests would be worth it. In short order the commands were carried out and the orderly was carrying his luggage up the winding stone stairway, wondering with every step of the way how the blind colonel would be able to negotiate it, but Erich had no trouble at all.

It took several workmen from town to break through the sealed heavy oak doors to get the room ready. Not only was the task of bringing that antique bed up the stairwell absolutely impossible, it turned out to be unnecessary. The room behind those doors was much larger than had been expected and it was completely furnished, including an antique bed exactly the same as the one below. It would take another day to install the electricity and telephone but these were not an immediate priority for the blind man. No one seemed to notice the fear that had taken hold of the Polish workmen when they were ordered to break into the room. The pneumatic tools that were needed pried the door loose and when it was forced open they expected to find the bones of the young baroness, lying in her bed along with her Jewish lover from the century before, when the doors were sealed. They said nothing about this to anyone, finished their work and were happy to escape with their lives.

The colonel rose early, to the cawing of the crows, went down to shower and dress and prepared for the day. His orderly brought up breakfast upon his return and remarked about the salt mine. He was told when the next shift would be arriving and arranged to meet it at the mine. He was led down into the cavern and he kept going further in when he asked the guide to describe the scene. "Just where were the guards in relation to the workers? How deep was the water? Where does the steam vent shoot from? Who has control of the lighting, the main switch, the auxiliary switch? Is there any alarm system?" The guide was amazed at the complexity of the questions and the rapidity with which the blind colonel posed them. How did he know there was a jet stream? Not every question was answered right then but answers were expected later that day. Pretty soon the colonel left the mine, soaking wet with hot salt air, hardly able to breathe. "How on earth can the general expect to get efficient return of product when the people are forced to work under such destructive conditions?" he thought. "It's a wonder there isn't more sabotage!" The trip back to the castle only took a few minutes but the pain in his chest needed more time to feel better. Then it struck him. The solution to the killings.

V

The colonel retired to his room and asked not to be disturbed until dinner. Despite the heaviness that he felt in his chest, he sat at his desk trying to remember the studies in chemistry that he had taken at the University. The molecular charts, the formulas, the equations that he had had no use for since then, slowly began to unravel. Acids, bases, salts, elements, solids, liquids, gases, byproducts, agents needed to cause reactions, then disappear, it all should confirm his suspicions but what was the clue that he needed. Now his head began to ache. He lay down in the bed with no intention of falling asleep but numbers and letters did their work, he was out cold. Nothing in his sleep helped him out of his dilemma. The evening shade had begun to veil the castle when his orderly knocked on the heavy oak door. Dinner was served, so he rose to the table that had been set up for him and invited the soldier to enter. The tray was set with hot food in the center as instructed. The salad was plain, with small dispensers of vinegar and oil to the left, the salt and pepper shaker to the right exactly in the same place, so the colonel would have no trouble finding them. "Danke!" he said as the soldier retreated and shut the door. The night light had been lit, as usual, not for him but for anyone else who had to see his way around the room. Erich began to eat the meal when it came to him. He took the salt shaker and doused the heavy spoon with salt. Shifting hands, he poured some vinegar into the spoon and waited as the mixture began to bubble, sending acrid fumes into his nose. He was performing a simple experiment that he had done in school a long time ago. The fumes were so strong that he had to drop the spoon into his dinner but that didn't matter. He saw from his experiment that some acid that would react with the salt, especially in an atmosphere of steam, could have killed the guards in the mine at just the exact moment when the shift of the Polish slaves was being transferred out and the other was being brought in. It had had to be strong enough acid to work quickly, fast enough to cause death by asphyxiation, yet not enough to linger and kill the Poles. Before he could finish his dinner he called the supply officer. The latter was very upset, being called away from his dinner in the Officers' Mess Hall but his answer was exactly what the colonel needed. Yes, they had gallons of sulfuric acid and yes, they had high-pressure spray guns, needed for fumigation. How the enemy got them and was able to use them was another mystery.

Whether the general would be happy or not with this news, he did not know. Maybe he would not divulge the news just yet. He knew that he could always stall. As a matter of fact, he decided to keep it from Helga, also. Somewhere there was a leak, so it would be wise not to trust anyone. The next day he would have a casual talk with the staff doctor to discuss the effect that hydrogen chloride gas could have on the pulmonary system. It was not clear how much poison would be effective over the area of the mine, its duration of effectiveness and why it was undetectable. The doctor appeared at the appointed time and the two men felt very comfortable with each other from the first handshake. Erich immediately got to the problem, which the doctor had been involved in before he arrived. His question was direct and the answer of the doctor was so simple. "We use sulfuric acid to recharge the fire extinguishers in the Shloss and in the mine as well. They are hung every fifty feet or so along the electric cable that keeps the lights on."

"Why didn't he see that sooner?" he asked himself. He had a few more questions regarding the autopsies. Standard questions, standard answers followed by some social chit chat. Both men rose. The colonel extended his hand, which the doctor grasped and then promised each other to keep in touch. The orderly, who escorted the colonel to the meeting, came to assist him on his way back to his office. As soon as he got settled he rang up Helga and had her send a memo to the chief engineer for a schematic of the electric system in the mine and the location of the fire extinguishers.

He had been on the right track, he was sure. Now the pieces began to fit together. The material he had requested confirmed his theory. Naturally, the sodium bicarbonate in the fire extinguisher produces carbon dioxide and water when it is inverted and the sulfuric acid in the little bottle mixes with it. Inside the canister a very high pressure is then produced, which shoots the mixture out of the hose and douses the flames. The C02 is not lethal as the HCL, so the sodium bicarbonate had to be replaced by the salt solution. "Yes!" he thought. "When the lights went out, the canisters were inverted and the hydrogen chloride mixed with the steamy salty air producing enough gas to kill the guards. Not just by asphyxiation but had the doctor thoroughly examined the lungs he would have found the burns from the hydrochloric acid. That was the product of combining with the steam. He reached across his desk, took up his pen and scribbled on his pad,

$$\mathrm{NaCI+H2S04= Na2S04+ 2HCI}$$

the essential ingredient in his report. Now that he knew what was done, the question was how the electric was conveniently shut off and by whom? A sergeant's uniform and I.D. would help the enemy gain access, but how did someone arrange the murders, themselves; the next question was what kind of electrical circuit did the mine have?

VI

As soon as Helga arrived, he asked her, "Is there a brauhaus in town? For a few seconds she was taken aback by the abruptness of the question. Usually, he would start the day with little amenities; at the least, he would let her sit down and get ready for work. She replied, "I never go there but I have heard that the old Jew tavern is being used as a beer hall for the troops. In the hot weather tables are set out back where the men drink beer and sing. After all, this is an army town. It's located in the lewd section." She hesitated, not knowing what the colonel had in mind or what he wanted to know.

He confided in her, "One of the enemies has been getting inside information. He may be dressed as one of our soldiers. Maybe we can set a trap. Helga, ring up personnel for me!"

The voice on the other end of the line answered, "Sheffer, here!"

"Is this personnel?" she asked, her smile affirmed that it was correct and she handed Erich the phone. He noticed how light it felt compared with the field telephones. In his sharp, official voice, he said, "This is Kolonel von Schmidt. Look up the file for the name and rank of that soldier that was killed in the salt mine and left naked. Get back to me as soon as you have it and be quick about it!" He slammed the receiver onto its cradle before a reply could be made. Helga had never seen him act this way before and she felt her admiration for him explode. The two sat there, silently, waiting for the return call. The few minutes seemed like an hour. They both jumped when the phone rang.

"Donner, Korporal Donner, sir. Lieutenant Sheffer told me that you wanted the file on Seargent Gruber, the victim of the salt mine incident. I have it here. Shall I ring it up?" "Does it have a photograph?" asked the colonel. With an affirmative from the other end, he ordered the soldier to make a photocopy of all the material and bring it to his office as soon as it was done. With the expected, "Yes, sir!" the phone was hung up again. He studied the report as though he could actually see it although Helga had read them to him. She could not understand why he would ask for a photograph but let it pass as something he was doing out of habit from before the accident. All of a sudden his voice changed with excitement, urgency.

"Get me the man in charge of RandR!" he ordered. Lieutenant Freuhoff answered the call and Erich commanded, "Tell him to get his butt up here, immediately!" A different man sat before her, a hunter, a trapper. No longer did she have feelings of sympathy for this blind soul. She began feeling a new sense of pride for having been assigned to the colonel.

The knock on the door came sooner than expected and the officer entered, standing at attention. not knowing where to go or what to do. Who was this colonel anyway? He had been in the middle of a delicate conversation with the lovely fraulein, Sergeant Rosa, when the call came. Helga had to stifle her laugh as she notices the lieutenant's fly was unbuttoned. Although she knew that the colonel couldn't see it, she signaled down to the open fly, which the officer deftly buttoned. When his salute received no reply, he approached the desk and said, "Sir, Lieutenant Freuhoff, sir!"

"Well, good!" Erich replied. "I need a favor, this weekend, I want all leaves canceled for sergeants, no matter what excuse you have to give them! Understood?" The answer, "Yes, sir!" was given a curt, "Dismissed!" and the lieutenant gave his salute to the bind man, made the perfect about face and departed. Before he reached the door, the colonel shouted at him, "Top secret!" From the other side of the door came the lieutenant's, "Yes, sir!" A lot of disgruntled sergeants were restricted to barracks on the pretext that a very valuable watch had been stolen and they were ordered to search the whole camp until it was found. It would be a surprise when it was found on Monday and so would be the catching of the phony sergeant spy.

The colonel had the M.P.s stake out the tavern and the "houses" all weekend long. He waited by the telephone all day and all night. He had his meals in his room. Helga kept the vigil with him until he ordered her to leave at night. Every time the phone rang, he jumped with anticipation. But he wasn't the only one waiting, the general was, too. What had gone wrong? Why hadn't the spy shown up? Had he been tipped off? Did he have access to the castle? Inside information?

The perfect snare had slipped. The general wasn't too upset; he knew that the colonel would succeed sooner or later. Erich sat in his chair, if he could see he would be staring into space. When Helga arrived he immediately got back to work.

He had many things to dictate and Helga had no trouble keeping up with him. Finally, he decided that they should stop and that they continue tomorrow. Helga put her things together. He was deep in thought; all the problems and solutions seemed to be flying around inside his head. He thought that he had heard her close the door. The lilac scent always lingered in the room after she left, but today it seemed stronger than usual. Had he heard the inside latch being closed or was it his imagination? He remembered hearing her footsteps going to the door but couldn't recall hearing it close behind her. His keen sense of hearing did not pick up the steps she made in her stocking feet because she deftly removed her shoes, after she had locked the door. He had removed his glasses, placing them before him on the desk and leaned onto his raised hands to rest his weary head, heaved a dreary sigh.

Helga's heart felt that it would burst. There was no way that she could stop herself. The blind Adonis had to make love to her or she would die. As she stepped slowly forward, she wished that he could see her drop her skirt, open her blouse and loosen the golden braid behind her neck. She couldn't understand why he didn't say something, do something. He surely must have heard her approach, noticed her scent. She couldn't stop. Something had possession of her. She moved around to the back of his chair and caressed his soft blond hair. An electric shock shot through her whole body. One of her hands stroked his ear, his neck, while the other undid her bra. Silently it fell behind her as she leaned forward, letting her ample breasts embrace his head, so warm and soft. Slowly, Erich laid his head back to receive her lips, hot and moist, reaching up to hold her face to his, strongly but gently. Slowly, as though a signal had been given, he rose from the leather chair. She gently led him toward the immense antique bed, opening his shirt, kissing him every step of the way. "What a perfect specimen of Aryan manhood he was. If only he could see what a perfect match she was for him, a union of the Gods!" she mused to herself. They had reached the bed and she sat beside him. He never said a word, nor did he have to. She could see his whole body speak in a language that was greater than mere words. The room was dark but it did not matter because he couldn't tell if it was or not. The thought of their being enveloped in each other, made their love-making soar to unimaginable heights.

She was not a tramp, light some of the other girls. While in youth camp, she had resisted the Feuhrer's orders, to have babies. It had to be love, for her, and this was it. This was right! The colonel continued to undress himself between the kisses. She helped him, as she had so often dreamed of doing. She couldn't wait! The love embrace was tender and fierce at the same time. He wouldn't see the stain on the sheet and she wouldn't tell him that he was the first. "How lucky I am!" she thought. She had found her Prince Charming, her Lohengrin, her Tristan!

"Mein Liebchen!" he whispered, and she responded with more kisses and more loving. Exhausted, they finally fell asleep. It was dark when she left his arms and dressed to leave. Silently, she let herself out and slipped down the spiral stairway. If it were possible, she would have flown. "How could anyone be so happy?" she kept saying to herself as she lay down on her bed. She hugged her pillow under her, over her, between her arms, between her legs. Sighing his name, she finally fell asleep.

The next morning, she arose, bright and early, even before the crows. A quick breakfast in the soldiers' mess hall. Some of her chums seemed to smile at her or was that her imagination. "Did it show?" she thought. Well, yesterday was yesterday. Today, her duty was to the Feuhrer! She knocked on the big oak door and the colonel called, "Enter!" Another day! There were more reports to be read, more material to record and type. She knew how important his work was and now there was more than one reason to be an efficient secretary.

Today, the colonel decided to venture down from his room, When Fritz saw him come into the kennel; the dog went into a frenzy. The harness was affixed and with his white cane in one hand and Fritz's harness in the other, the colonel walked out into the bright sunlight of Watermill. The sentries saluted him and cheered as he made his way down the path and out of the gate on his way toward town. Erich made his way along the road as surefooted as any sighted man. The officers and soldiers alike stopped in disbelief at seeing the colonel move so rapidly with his guide dog. They were confused about whether to salute and when they did, how did the colonel know to respond? They were surprised to see him headed toward the tavern and the bawdy houses, in broad daylight. Surely an officer of his rank could have had any lady, any army girl, for the asking. His asking directions to the Madame Maryushka's house was strange indeed. He raised his cane and knocked three times, paused and knocked twice again. Was it a coincidence or a signal?

The door sprung open and he entered. The door shut as quickly as it was opened and he stood in the room for a few minutes to acclimate himself to the darkness of the interior. Slowly, he walked over to the old fashioned round walnut table and sat down. Fritz lay down beside him as he folded his white cane and set it on the table. The young lady silently stood before him, waiting for him to speak. "A light shown in the window!" he slowly recited. Then he waited for her reply. In the same deliberate speech, she replied, ". . . and the crow flew away with the dove!"

The mystery of that sentence lay in something that happened a long time ago, but it was now the password needed to establish the recognition of a partisan. Erich rose and pushed his dark glasses onto his head and said as he moved toward her embrace, ". . . and the baron died with his grief" When they separated she took some tea from the copper samovar. As he sucked in the delicious aroma and hearty flavor of the beverage of his youth, he let out a sigh. For the first time in a long while he felt at home.

"Well, Slomovitch," she finally said. "I've been waiting for you for a month. What's been keeping you? No don't answer! Now that you are here, it doesn't matter." She had taken a seat close to him so she could study his strong face, his sky-blue eyes and blond hair. What a fine specimen of German manhood he represented, she thought. What a fine specimen of Polish womanhood she was, so plump, and pale; the blossom of rosy cheeks made her look younger than she really was. Anything that he would propose she was sworn to do and now she waited to find out what orders he was going to give. She had spoken in Polish although her German had become quite fluent. After all, the business demanded it.

The colonel answered in perfect Polish, as easily as he could have in German. "I'm going to arrange for you to visit me for sexual favors. That way we'll be able to get together without any suspicion and without interruption. Having you, the attractive Madame of Watermill, come to my bed will be easy to arrange. Your access to the Shloss will not be questioned once our relationship is established. That way we'll be able to exchange information in both directions. The candle will be lit in the window and everyone who sees it will know that you are coming for a liaison with the blind colonel. By the way, do you have anything for me?"

"No, except the next train will be derailed north of Pilski. The Germans are arranging a decoy, so we're arranging a double surprise!" He rose, returning his dark glasses to his face, taking up his white stick and Fritz's harness and turned to leave. "Auf Weidersehn!"

"Dasvidanya!" she said with her beautiful smile.

VII

How and where the switch had been made only the lieutenant and the Red Army brass actually knew. As soon as he reached his room, he set about attaching his transmitter to one of the forest of antennas above his roof. The equipment would stay hidden in the secret alcove that no one knew about. That his mother knew of the secret alcove in the Shloss was itself a mystery. She had told him that somewhere in the family history the Shloss of Watermill and the secret alcove had played an important role in the long past. Just before he had left for this assignment she had confided to him that he was a Jew and his roots were in Watermill. He had never been registered as one and had not been circumcised, like so many of his peers. Under Stalin it was all but impossible. Then again, he thought, Helga would surely have questioned him about it. The charade would continue.

Late that night, the door securely latched, he sent his first message, the troop train derailment would not come as a surprise to the Soviet high command or the underground. If the plan worked the derailment would kill a regiment of a crack Panzer Division, officers included. The sergeant on duty in message center, running through his receiver to pick up short-wave news from Berlin, caught the strange transmissions coming from the Shloss. He began to copy the encoded message signal. "Da Da, Dit Dit Da, Dit Da" and at the end a long Da. He ran it through his code manual. Not a clue. He couldn't decide whether or not to give the copy to his superior or let it go. He had been in enough hot water when some of the message center slips with his signature had been found near the brothels in town. By some fluke he had avoided a court martial when the garbage truck from the Shloss passed through town and some of the old message-center slips had blown off into the street, exonerating him. While he was musing over his choice, the coded signal started up again. He decided not to pursue it, adjusting his headset and flipping the dial until he caught Radio Berlin.

The colonel finished his work, carefully stashed the equipment in the secret alcove and went to sleep. The general was happy that the "murders" in Watermill had stopped and his field operations were moving ahead according to plan. Well, it wasn't exactly Drei Nacht Oesten but nothing was happening that was critical. He was not faulted for the bridge collapse in Pilski. The army engineers had reported that it was metal fatigue that was the cause. In truth they were covering themselves for neglecting to find the problem before the truck convoy was destroyed. No one would acknowledge that the partisans had succeeded in their sabotage. He crawled into his bed confident that his friend von Schmidt, was taking care of matters in his room upstairs. It was going to be a good night, he mused. A light rain had begun to fall, giving the Shloss a foreboding appearance of gloom and doom. The train was taking a circuitous route to avoid tracking by the Underground. Another identical train in size and appearance took the direct route. If the timing were perfect the traffic controller would have masterminded a fool proof system to safely transport the troops. But the transmission was sent to the Shloss and picked up by the partisans, unknown to him. Charges of dynamite were set and fuses fixed. The idea was to destroy the decoy as well as the real troop train.

They were getting periodic information from the station masters, pinpointing all the trains' locations. At 03:00 plus seven the action would commence. The men and women were stationed with their German Shmeissers, loaded and ready. The Polish engineer cautiously moved ahead. One toot on the horn. The armed soldier in the cab shouted over the din of the engine. The engineer motioned that he could not hear. The fuses were lit as the train came into sight. All the soldiers, except the ones that were on guard duty, were asleep. The steep grade ahead forced the train to slow to a crawl. The charges were greater than ever before amassed. Next to the bridge at Pilski, this would set a record. Most of the blasts went off enough to damage the rails and some of the cars, but it was not as much as had been planned. The light rain had soaked into the fuses and killed the igniting flames. In a flurry of excitement the troops, half naked, were out of the train, deploying with their weapons hunting down the enemy. Most escaped; some were caught and shot on the spot. Rrrrring! The general didn't let the second ring come. Even when he picked up the phone he knew it had to be bad news. He listened half asleep.

"Ja! Ja!" a pause and another "Ja!" Then he slammed the receiver back on its cradle. "Thank G-d for the rain," he thought. Well maybe his luck is changing. They said that they caught the leader, a man they called, "The Crow." Let the Gestapo handle this mess. He turned over and settled into sleep. Rrrrrring!

"Gott in himmel!" he screamed. He stabbed blindly at the phone, knocking it onto the floor so the receiver was pulled away from his ear. He cursed the Fench phone as he strained to hear the voice at the other end. "Ja!" The voice at the other end reported the bad news. Herr General," (with a hard "G") "the decoy was completely demolished!"

The general snorted, "Gut!" and hung up, leaving the caller completely confused. "Why was this happening to him, here in this peaceful idyllic valley, Watermill," he asked out loud. He tried to fall asleep but was too upset. He was worried about Berlin and the Gestapo.

The following morning the Gestapo descended on the wreck like flies on a corpse, looking for clues. The Crow had been taken to the Magistrate and torturing him had begun immediately. It may have been futile but brutality bolstered their ego. At the scene, of the explosion the unexploded dynamite gave evidence that army ordinance had been robbed at a significant rate. The general would pay for his indifference and neglect of security, which only the Gestapo could satisfactorily provide. He would pay for making the Shloss off limits to them. This was their time. At least there were no casualties and the troops would be on their way as soon as the rails were repaired.

All through the night the soldiers from the train deployed searching for guerrillas who seemed to vanish in the mist. At the break of dawn the general dispatched wrecking crews and Polish rail workers to repair the damage and waited for a backup train to arrive. An assessment of the damage let the general off the hook, again. Just a delay of two days and the crack troops would be on their way again.

Well, the troops were not killed by the enemy. The antennas above the Shloss were crackling with messages to and from the front. The general's war room was buzzing with activity. Never had the Shloss seen such a frenzy. The colonel was listening to Helga reading the reports. Whatever had happened a few days before between them had to be shunted aside. In the heat of the moment she began addressing him as "Herr Kolonel" again. He didn't object. He thought about The Crow and was sorry that the Black and Skulls had taken him. He was confident that The Crow wouldn't talk even if they killed him. If only he hadn't delayed, trying to help a wounded comrade, he would have escaped. An idea flashed through Erich's brain but that would have to wait until that night.

Most people in town never noticed the tiny candle burning in the window but Maryushka did. Although almost every one of the Germans in the Shloss knew her and used her girls, none ever remembered her coming to the Shloss. This night she came up to the sentry wearing a gorgeous embroidered peasant blouse pulled seductively down around her shoulders. Her golden hair was pinned up to reveal her long regal neck and tiny ears hung with jeweled earrings. Although she spoke German she pretended not to and in Polish she indicated that she had a date with Kolonel Von Schmidt. The sentry shrugged that he didn't understand Polish so she pushed against him, pursing her lips and whispering, "Von Sh-Sh!"

"Herr Kolonel von Schmidt?" the young man finally understood.

"Ja!, Ja!" she smiled radiantly as he opened the huge oak doors to let her enter. The officer of the day gave her a pass and showed her to the stairway that led to the colonel's apartment. He clicked his heels and bowed as she began to ascend. When he returned to his post he could see the other officers. With their approving smiles, congratulating the colonel upon his good taste. "At least the colonel's accident had not cost him his manhood when he lost his sight," they all thought. She scurried up the long winding stairwell intermittently set with electric lamps. The doors flung open as soon as she knocked and were slammed shut as soon as she entered. "How did you manage to get in so quickly?" he asked, removing his glasses. As quickly she replied, "You're not the only intelligence here!" With a smile on his handsome face, he replied, "Here's what we have to do! We know that Crow is in the dungeon at the Magistrate. They will surely kill him. Get a message to him so we can find a sergeant's uniform. If it's Crow's so be it. If not it's as well."

After a pause she asked, "Is that all?"

"Yes!" came his blunt reply.

With a smile, she said, "Well, I can't leave now. Our assignation should last at least an hour. The walls and the doors are so thick that no one would hear us even if we pretended." Maryushka sat back in the chair that Helga uses and decided to pass the remaining time by telling Josef the history of the Shloss, of the young baroness and the tailor's son. Little did he realize that it was a story about his own ancestors, many generations ago. Before they knew it, more than two hours had passed and they decided for her to leave. Just before he opened the latch, she gave him a hug, tousseled her hair, wiped the lipstick off her mouth, and adjusted her blouse to make it look disheveled.

"How do I look?" she asked, adopting a seductive pose.

"Like a real hussy!" he replied. The words in German sounded mean, but she understood. Down the stairs she flew, blowing kisses to the soldiers on the way out of the Shloss and down the path and through the gate on her way home. All the way she kept praying that The Crow would live long enough to allow her to fulfill her mission. She had to get the message to Ivan, the caretaker of the Magistrate. Luck was with them and a sergeant's uniform was delivered to her home. A witness would confess to Colonel Erich that he had found the uniform, tying it to The Crow and the salt mine murders. He would have the general gain Crow's release from the Gestapo so that he could get a full confession about the Underground. That would put the general in good standing with the Wehrmacht and save Crow from more brutal punishment.

After much haggling and arguing about authority, The Crow was released to the custody of the colonel, where he lingered between life and death, a broken body but not a broken spirit. All attempts were made to keep him alive but the Gestapo brutes were too thorough. Finally when the body was removed from the Shloss, Maryushka arranged a hero's burial somewhere in the woods, with his comrades attending his last rites, beneath the Carpathian Mountains that he loved. The priest from the Watermill church said the Mass with tears of grief choking his every word and the small group of partisans stood there solemnly vowing to avenge his death. Who could replace The Crow, the patriot, the fighter, the man?

Back in the castle, the colonel was preparing an elaborate memo, telling all about the undercover work which had been arranged by him to solve the great mystery. Now that the sergeant-spy, who had eluded all other intelligence, was finally gone and the mysterious deaths in the salt mine, which hung over the general like Damocles' sword, were solved, the atmosphere in the Shloss at Watermill became routine. The colonel was not only credited with solving the "Crow" case and the Sergeant case, he was also getting credit for the cessation of sabotage. The general prepared a citation honoring Erich and was proposing another medal for his already bedecked chest.

Military secrets were hard to glean in the Shloss. Being confined to his quarters except for the time he walked Fritz around the compound, the colonel was able to make very little contact with what went on in the war room. He still had to rely on Maryushka and her band of spies. The sex business was good and although no money changed hands, the gifts of food and wine were generous. In fact there was food enough to distribute to most of the local slave labor and the partisans. The tavern was a wealth of information and so were the brothels. Love and alcohol were the keys to reports and orders that only the general's top staff were privy to. So the candle in the window sparkled almost every night and sexy Maryushka came to the Shloss to entertain the blind colonel.

"When is the wedding day?" they teased her. Little did they suspect that nothing sexual was going on. Only one person was really bothered by these visits and it was Helga. Not since that first time they had been intimate had anything happened between them. She burned with desire and she burned with jealousy. He had become very official, never letting down his guard. He had even asked her to stop wearing the lilac scent that she loved to wear, during working hours. She waited with hope that her colonel would return to her. She would hide in the entrance area and watch as the gorgeous Polish blond would toy with the men on her way to the spiral stairway. She would torment herself with images of the colonel and the prostitute in that immense bed. But her first duty was to the Feuhrer, so she had to hide her feelings and do her job.

VIII

Every other night the antenna above the Shloss crackled with a secret code. The message center knew it, the Gestapo knew it, but no one realized that it was a coded message that only the Kremlin could decipher. The transmissions were only one-way. The colonel really had no way of knowing if his work was being received or not and, even if it was, whether it was useful to his government. Well, that wasn't his business, was it? The weather was still warm and the Nazi juggernaught was still moving steadily into Russia. What would happen to his beloved home, his family, his friends? Maybe the messages that he has been sending were helping, but from the news reports he had doubts. Whatever, this was his role in the war and he would do his duty for the motherland. If he got home safely, he would get the Lenin Medal of Honor and a promotion. Premier Stalin had told him so himself when he shook his hand. "Slomovitch," he said, "The Great Mother Russia needs your help!" They all took up their shnapps glasses and saluted with a hearty "Nazdrovya!" and downed the 200-proof vodka. Why was all this running through his mind undermining his confidence? He shrugged it off and got to work.

Whenever Maryushka had some valuable information for him she dressed up seductively and met with the colonel. With the war moving further away, the control center had to be moved closer to the front. The general and his staff moved out of the Shloss but he left behind a skeleton crew and the message center because their radio transmitters to Berlin headquarters were more powerful. It was also the final decision of the Wehrmacht to leave a message center here in Watermill which was useful for its rail depot and salt mines. The colonel's secret work would be able to continue but the need for his intelligent expertise obviously became less important. The Gestapo was getting very nosey, now that the general was in the field. Several of the "girls" were taken in for interrogation. When they returned, their whole personality had changed. Their "joie de vivre" was gone. They showed signs of paranoia. They were not desirable anymore. Maryushka was having trouble with them. They were asked about her visits to the Shloss and she was afraid that they might have slipped up and made the Gestapo suspicious. Perhaps someone in the Shloss was spying on them.

It was becoming obvious that Helga was getting more and more jealous of her visits. She began to follow Maryushka, blatantly calling vile names after her. The Madame pretended not to understand the German words, smiling innocently in her direction, but even if she didn't understand, the tone of Helga's voice made pretty obvious her obsession for Erich. Maryushka confessed all this to him on her visit and they had to figure out some way to change things.

During some of the hours when he was alone, with the doors latched shut, he ventured down the secret passageway that was hidden behind the alcove, where he kept the transmitter. His electric torch led him through a labyrinth of passages under the Shloss and took him to a trap door far out on the hill behind the castle. This he told Maryushka, had to be the way for her to meet him from now on. They would stage an argument that night in front of the personnel. Everyone, including Helga, would know that the colonel and the lady were through. When the candle was lit in the window the secret trap door was to be used. Maryushka was happy to come but she had less to report to him. When the soldiers and material moved to the front, so did the Underground activities. The tavern was going bankrupt even though the beer was coming from the army commissary. The love houses were shutting down for lack of business. Everything was changing in Watermill. The Gestapo had taken over the town. It would not be long before all the pieces were fit together and their secret operation would be uncovered.

The colonel had begun monitoring messages from the message center more closely. He confided to Maryushka that he was following the coded Gestapo messages to Berlin and they were awaiting orders from Heidrich to move against the whole town for their aid to the partisans. They had taken pieces of the Pilski Bridge and found evidence of tampering. Maryushka's face became white with fear.

What would happen to her girls, to her town, to her people?" she asked half to him, half to herself. Erich said he was working on a plan of evacuation right under the nose of the Gestapo. She would get the priest to lead a pilgrimage to the cathedral in Pilski. The army would supply the vehicles for transporting all of the girls, he would arrange for that. From there they would flee to the woods or scatter to other towns around the city. The other Poles would also disappear for the same religious reason. The word would come from the church that after the pilgrimage a great feast would be held in Watermill to honor the patron saint of Poland and everyone would be invited. Hopefully, the Gestapo would not get tipped off by anyone.

He escorted her down the steps and through the labyrinth under the Shloss. For the first time he could feel the cold sweat of her hand, the tremble of fear. He tried to assure her but his voice held a doubt that it never had before. As he kissed her forehead, for the first time he had allowed such an emotion between them, he whispered that everything would be all right, if it's G-d's will. He stood at the trap door and followed her with his eyes into the dark night until she disappeared. She carried the whole evacuation plan on her shoulders. How was she to know that Lieutenant Rosten, a Gestapo plainclothes officer, was observing her exit from the secret trap door. He did not follow her or arrest her; after all he knew where to find her when he wanted to and it was a good thing, too.

IX

When Maryushka used the front entrance to the castle it did not raise the suspicion of the Gestapo, but an army sentry in the field behind the Shloss had noticed her walking out there, then suddenly disappearing in the grass. He informed his army superior, who laughed at him and called him crazy, hallucinating. So he went to the Magistrat and talked to the Gestapo, who advised him to say nothing to anyone else. They would look into the matter. The Gestapo lieutenant told no one either but decided to take up surveillance out behind the old castle, himself. It would be a coup for him if he alone exposed some anti-Nazi conspiracy. From his secret outpost he noticed that on certain nights a candle was lit in the window way at the top of the tower even though the electric lamps were lit. And why were the lamps lit in the tower when everyone knew that the Kolonel was blind as a bat? The sentry did not even know that he was there every night stalking her. He would show up those corrupt Gestapo officers in the Magistrate who treated him like a mere peasant. He himself would find out what his superiors could not. They would be forced to promote him to rank befitting a hero in the Black and Skull. Although Rosten was off duty that day; he would keep an eye on the Kolonel as he took his dog Fritz by the harness for his walk out of the compound. In order to account for the Kolonel's routine, he had to check everything, so he recorded the time on his chronometer into his little black book. Well done. the Kolonel will be gone from the castle at least forty-five minutes according to his schedule, enough time for him to do a little investigating. He ran around to the field behind the castle and removed the camouflaged steel trap door. "Had anyone seen him?" he wondered. He waited three minutes. Clear! His electric torch led him through the labyrinth and up the stairwell. On the ledge at the top he was shocked by what he saw.

"Vass iss dass?" he shouted out loud, getting back the question in an echo from the walls below him. "Ach! Ja!" he muttered as he realized that he found the clue to the mystery code transmissions that had baffled his superiors. The brand name had been removed from the instrument but some of the cues to operation were in Russian. Something was obviously dead wrong! he realized. He didn't touch a thing. He squeezed through the alcove to the colonels quarters, checked out the desk, some papers and the massive bed. What a shame that he had to sleep on an army cot, he thought. Suddenly he realized that there were sounds of the heavy latches being opened outside of the huge oak doors. "Mein Gott!" he said to himself. "He has cut his walk short!" A woman's voice was speaking German as the doors were opened. He couldn't make out the muffled words nor did he dare to tarry. He had found his spy, his Mata Hari, his evidence. He slithered down the secret stairway, through the labyrinth and out the trap door just in time. Going from the black tunnel into the bright sunlight of the field stunned his eyes as he staggered away from the castle.

Several nights passed and Rosten saw no light in the window, no figure disappearing down the trap door. He decided to tell his superiors nothing. Why should they get the honors for his detective work? When it was a 'fait accompli' he would give in his full report and make copies so that they could not make a claim to his success. The next night he did notice the signal in the window way at the top of the Shloss. The figure of a woman slid into view and suddenly disappeared. He could wait for her to come down from the tower, confront her in the field and force her at gunpoint back up to the colonel's rooms. Using her as a hostage he would confront the blind Kolonel von Schmidt, get the truth from him and then shoot them both, thus avoiding any complications. "Dead people don't offer too much resistance!" he chuckled to himself. Not only would he have caught the spy network, he would also show that the people of Watermill were conspirators and the stupid army was a party to it all. Under his orders, the Gestapo would round up all the women and men of Watermill and finish the job that they had done with the Jews. He smiled to himself, "Two trenches, side by side. How efficient!" He waited until dawn but the woman had not come out. Had he been so busy musing about success that he had missed her? Well, there would be another night when he would catch his bird. Then the candle was lit again.

It wasn't until the middle of the night that he saw his quarry before him. He forgot his original plan to wait and rushed forward, his Luger in his hand, cocked and ready. "Halt!" he shouted. The lady stopped cold. He commanded her to approach but she didn't understand German. He motioned with the barrel of the gun. She understood that. Yes, just as he had guessed. The beautiful Madame of Watermill. It was no use to confront her, she wouldn't understand his German and he wouldn't understand her Polish. The pistol would have to do the talking. He motioned her toward the trap door. It was the tone of his voice rather than the word, "Shnell!" that made her move rapidly. The only thought on her mind was, "How can I warn, Josef?" Stealthily they walked through the labyrinth and up the stairs. The space was too narrow for him to keep his hand over her mouth but the muzzle in her back did the trick. The colonel was expecting her so he showed no surprise when they burst into the room from the alcove.

"Mein Herr Kolonel!" his voice constricted and sharp. Rosten had learned how to sound authoritarian from his superiors. "You are under arrest for spying against the Feuhrer and the Third Reich!" Erich didn't move. He could see the Luger in Maryushka's spine.

"You're crazy!" he protested. "I'm a decorated Kolonel in the Wehrmacht! I'll have you shot for this!"

"Oh, no!" replied Rosten. "On the contrary, not I but you will be shot. Not you but I will be a decorated hero when they see your Russian transmitter, Herr Russian spy." Erich reached for his white cane but the Gestapo man thought he was reaching for a gun. The flame shot from the Luger and the colonel pitched forward onto the desk, his crimson blood spreading over the papers, the color of his beloved Soviet flag. Maryushka screamed, then fell silent as the bullet pierced her heart. No one in the Shloss heard the shots. The thick stone walls and heavy oak doors barred the sound from the rest of the castle. Only the black crows heard the crack of the gun. They flew out of their nests screaming, made one pass around the castle and settled down again to sleep. The candle was still burning in the window when Rosten opened the doors and strode down the spiral stairway to make the call to the Magistrat. Single-handedly he had met the enemy and destroyed them.

He was startled awake by a rustling sound. It must have been the breeze. He had fallen asleep on his watch. It was later than he thought, checking his chronometer. He must have missed the lady coming in to the trap door. He would catch her coming out. He did not see Maryushka but she had seen him as he stretched and wiped the sleep from his eyes. Before he knew it the blade of her knife had pierced his ribcage and his heart. She dragged the body over to the trap door and dropped it into the hole, not even bothering to cover it.

X

It used to be said, "Passionate men often boast, drunken men brag!" The German command thought it was mere coincidence that their advancing troops were met with flames instead of food. The scorched-earth policy looked like random acts of patriotism to them. The Russian peasants knew that it was a military program to impede the advancing German army and deny them the spoils of war. Josef's messages made last-minute maneuvers against the enemy possible because secrets only the German staff knew were getting to the Kremlin. The cold black walls seemed to radiate warmth when beautiful Maryushka stepped from the alcove. Did Josef notice what she felt? She disciplined herself. She chastised herself. He was a Russian officer, probably married and a Christian, she thought. She could not betray her oath to avenge the murder of her people. She must not get involved with him.

The German officers and soldiers were just men, serving their country, patriots, but Maryushka would have liked to kill them all, dead, murdered, like the massacred men and women who lay cold and rotting in the trench behind the tavern. Their revelry, their robust singing, their cheers as they lifted the steins of brew, chanting their Horst Wessel hymn, made her heart ache. Yet they were the channel, the conduit from which she could do her work, her part. Passionate men often bragged and drunken men even bragged more. The men stationed in Watermill felt as though they were deprived of their highest duty to the Feuhrer. The guns they carried were not hot with the fire of combat. Little did they know that their troops were beginning to freeze in the winter of the east.

Erich sat at his desk, weary, the door bolted. Helga was gone for the night. He pushed aside the encoded messages that he would have to transmit later, shut his eyes and leaned back in his chair. He had heard through the grapevine that his city had been overrun. What could he have done to save it? This whole Watermill could fit into one section of his beloved city. What had happened to his family, friends? Had they been able to escape? Had the messages he had sent been of any help in their evacuation or had the pincer movements of the Germans entrapped them?

The following morning the colonel looked at Helga. She didn't realize he could see her; after all his dead eyes lay hidden behind those black lenses he wore. How different she was from Maryushka, he mused. Helga thought that he was collecting his thoughts, preparing the next paragraph that she had to write. The supple warm maiden had turned to stone cold as the gray stone of the Shloss. She seemed more erect, more official. It was obvious that she had turned from love to hate because of Maryushka. He must never let down his guard, never! The braid which used to be loose and youthful was now worn so tightly it looked like a noose. Her ample breasts were bound so tightly in her uniform blouse that she almost looked masculine. Even her voice had become sharp and military. He was brought back to the task by her military tone, "Herr Kolonel, sir!" Later, he sent a message for Maryushka to come through the front. Despite the terrible burden that Maryushka carried, she never seemed to lose her warmth. In his presence she exuded charm and wit. The visits, at first, were longer and had to reflect a meeting of a sexual nature. The meetings that occurred when she came through the trap door were shorter, just for business. Occasionally he would ask a question, seemingly about Watermill, but actually it was to find out about her. He was also interested in learning about the Shloss, how old it was and why it had been closed and abandoned for generations.

At first she was reluctant but as her confidence grew she offered more and more information. Much of what she knew, she explained, was from what her grandmother had told her as a child and much of her knowledge had passed on from her parents and so forth. So Maryushka began to tell the strange story of the Shloss to the colonel. Again it was being passed on as it had been done for generations. She began the story with the arrival of the tailor from Pilski with his pregnant wife. The tailor had a terrible stutter. Upon their arrival her great-great grandfather who worked in the tavern took them in and that very night their baby girl was born. She soon died and was buried behind the tavern. There used to be a small stone where she was buried. The marker was destroyed by the Nazis after years of being preserved. Soon after the tragedy, the couple set up a tailor shop and after a while, had a baby boy who grew up big and handsome. They said that he had eyes as deep as the sky and hair as white as the snow.

"Grandma" she said, "was very poetic!" The story goes on to tell of the local baron and baroness who lived in this Shloss and who had a beautiful baby girl. The baroness died in childbirth but the girl looked just like her, with raven black hair and eyes as dark as night. When she came of age, her father arranged for her to marry a nobleman whom she didn't like because she had fallen in love with the tailor' son.

"I don't know all the details, but there was something to do with a candle in the window. That's why the signal between us seemed so amazing." The baron had been so incensed by his daughter's rebellion that he had her entombed in this very room. The tailor's son, unknown to him, was with her when the doors were sealed. Forever, it was believed that they died here and that the crows that fly about the Shloss are their spirits. When the Germans opened the sealed doors and especially this room, it seems that they escaped through the alcove and trap door. That was it. It was good that the heavy stone walls and the heavy oak door muted their laughter. All that night the colonel couldn't sleep. Something about her story kept churning up memories from his childhood, long past. He had been brought up in a nursery and had learned very little from his family. Yet something seemed to be trying to come out of his past. He heard a voice, perhaps that of his grandfather, an old man who spoke Yiddish with his grandmother, a language long lost to the Russian Jews. Yes! he was hearing the voice of that endearing old man, a tailor by trade, a scholar by desire, the wise old man that he loved.

Grandpa's voice, he remembered, smiling to himself, also told him a story of a far away castle and a princess who fell in love with a tailor's son. They were supposed to be put to death in the king's castle but they escaped through a passage with the help of a devoted governess. The boy had blue eyes and blond hair and the girl had black hair and eyes as dark as night. How strange it was that Maryushka's story about the Shloss seemed so similar to what he now was remembering. Grandma used to stand him and his sister before her on their visits and with loving embraces tease them about his white hair and her black. Of course little Josef always thought it was a fairy tale because stories about kings and princesses were discouraged in the Soviet Union. He began to nod when Helga' knock startled him awake.

"Ein moment, bitte!" he shouted, forgetting that his voice could not penetrate the door. He quickly checked around the room. There must never be the slightest clue that Helga might pick up on. Although he never slept late, she noticed his breakfast tray still outside the door. She checked the thermos and found that it was still piping hot although the toast was ice cold. "Well," she thought, "That Polish whore must have an orgy last night. Stop it!" she ordered herself. "Stop torturing yourself" but she couldn't. She kept seeing him, his tender but strong embrace. He was her German god and would always be; after all he was her first lover, her only love. When he finally undid the latch on the heavy oak door, she was gone and so was the tray. He sat down at his desk, again scanning the room for some telltale sign. He had just begun to relax when there was another knock. The latch was off and Helga entered the room with the tray balanced on one hand and the notebook snugly held under arm.

"Guten tag, mein Herr!" she chirped, a smile on her face. What happened that caused this change? As she moved across the room toward the desk she checked out the room for any telltale sign of a night of romance but everything was in order, everything was perfect, almost too perfect. "No!" she thought. She wouldn't tell her boss what she suspected, at least not yet, not without evidence. She took her seat before him, his beautiful smile sending shock waves through her whole body. The things were quiet around Watermill, the partisans were busy harassing the troops in the east and except for occasional sabotage of the railroad, which was under the jurisdiction of the Gestapo, and there was little intelligence for him to work on. The colonel asked some questions of Helga.

She had come from Bavaria near the Berchtesgarten. She was the youngest of seven children and two of her brothers had given their lives for the Reich in the Afrika Corps with Rommel. The others were somewhere, she didn't know. She swelled with pride as she talked about them and their dedication to the Fatherland. Her mother was a nursery school teacher; her father, a former university professor, was now a military instructor in Berlin.

"What else would you like to know?" she asked curtly as though he was questioning her credentials.

"Fraulein Helga!" he began.

"Korporal Helga!" she interrupted, correcting him.

He corrected himself, leaving out her name. "Korporal. If all Germans would be as honorable as your family our Feuhrer's plan would soon be a reality!"

Again she interrupted him. "It will be soon, Her Kolonel!"

He dismissed her until tomorrow morning. He was so tired. Why chance her interrogating him? What if she had seen his dossier and started to ask questions about him?

XI

The next time that she came to the Shloss it was through the labyrinth. It was then that Maryuhka confided in Josef that her real name was Miriam, something that her mother had told her shortly before the roundup and slaughter. Her parents had inherited the tavern that had been handed down for generations from a Nathan and Naomi. She was Jewish but vaguely, having been brought up in modern Poland. Because she was blond and blue-eyed her Polish friends at school overlooked her occasional participation in Jewish ritual or that she didn't wear a cross or attend Catholic Church. She learned enough about their religion not to alienate her classmates. Many Poles harbored anti-Semitic hatred, especially around Easter time when the old bishop agitated the people with Passion Plays, but not as overt as in centuries past.

She was accepted in the community, as was her family. In fact Maryushka was a favorite among her peers, many of whom she now enlisted in her clandestine pleasure houses. She was concerned that after the war, she and her ladies would be accused of collaboration with the enemy. "What they were able to do to help fight the Nazis had to be her first concern!" she constantly convinced herself. As for herself, it was their way to avenge the murder of her people and the enslaved Poles. After the war they would be seen as heroes.

He smiled as she spoke, her eyes belying the the strength of her words. When she was finished, she apologized for her long emotional talk. "Miriam," he repeated several times. Somewhere in his memory there was that name and the name

Chaim. It was too much of a coincidence that these names and stories could have come from both their pasts. They checked their watches at exactly the same moment. She decided to leave before dawn. She moved toward the alcove, not even waiting to say good-bye. She was gone. She needed no scent for her presence to linger. He too had to discipline himself, his thoughts, his desires. His mission was coming to an end. He set up the coding equipment and the transmitter for the last time. Tonight his message would be short and he would sign off. His work was of little value to the war effort and the Gestapo was getting close. He could not continue and jeopardize the people who helped him.

XII

The next day Helga asked him how he had lost his sight. It was sudden and it seemed that she was trying to catch him off guard. He tried to dismiss it with a curt remark.

"It's a long story, you wouldn't be interested." He could have told her what he had been briefed about the real Kolonel von Schmidt but he felt he didn't owe her an explanation. She insisted that she would be very interested, forcing a smile that she knew he was not able to see. Somehow she sounded more like a Gestapo interrogator than a secretary. Should he fabricate a story or tell the truth? He smiled and settled into a relaxed position. "Are you taking notes?" he asked jokingly. "Of course!" came her reply.

He found it hard to read her. One day, "Herr Kolonel!" and the next a friendly smiling charm. Perhaps she was actually counter-intelligence. "What a ploy!" he thought.

"I was on a ski-training operation in the Alps when I was called on to infiltrate the Kunstfarein, the radical artist colony, the hellhole where anti-German intrigue was being organized.

The Gestapo could never infiltrate this group the way I was able to. My univesity training in art gave me perfect credentials for fitting in. I hated every minute of it but it was a direct order from Himmler. To cut it short, I found a cache of weapons and dynamite. The booby trap was so unique that no one would have suspected it except the one who set it. The explosion was tremendous. I was thrown across the room by the blast. The next thing I knew was that I was in a hospital in Bonn, in pain and in the dark, and that is it." Did he detect a sniffle coming from the iron maiden? What would happen if she was able to get a copy of his dossier and read about the chemical explosion in the laboratory. "Well, what should she expect from an intelligence officer? The truth?" he thought.

The next day Helga didn't smell like lilacs but like the Gestapo. Her questions the day before seemed friendly compared with her attitude today. She seemed to have listed questions that would verify his story. She asked him about the Bauhaus, the German artists of Dada and modern expressionism, the work Hitler condemned as decadent, Communist, vile and corrupt. He parried each question and finally, becoming weary he asked sharply, "Any other questions, Korporal? I'm feeling a headache!" He dismissed her remarking, "It feels like a lovely day to take Fritz for a walk." He heard her close the door. Her quick steps down the stairs indicated her feeling successful in putting the mighty colonel under pressure. Why should she be the only one to suffer. He wondered, "Was she headed to the Gestapo or her commanding officer or neither?" He lay down on the bed. Needed to think. He had no idea of falling asleep. Rrrrrring! Rrrrrring! He was jarred awake. "Why the hell does the damn thing do that all the time?" he muttered to himself. He sat up and reached for the receiver. "Ja!" he whispered. The voice at the other end was distant and unfamiliar.

"Reich Marshall JodI, here!" My G-d, the top brass was calling him. His mind snapped to attention, he cleared his throat and answered.

"Ja Vohl, mein Herr Marshal!" What would this Prussian advisor to the Feuhrer want with him? Some static was interfering.

"Hello! Can you hear me clearly? These damn French phones . . ." came from the phone.

The colonel answered affirmatively. The marshal announced that Erich had been highly recommended to the Fuehrer for a special assignment and he must leave for Berlin immediately.

A "Heil Hitler!" followed and before the colonel could say a word the phone clicked off. He slammed the receiver down, "Damn," he mumbled to himself, "That's all I need, now!"

Since the massacre and the mass burial of the people, Maryushka hadn't paid attention to the weather except when it had to do with her work. Today was an especially overcast day, like an omen of something terrible. If she had a Jewish calendar she might have noticed that it was Tisha B'Av, a day of mourning for her ancestors. It meant nothing to her, the anniversary of the Temple's destruction, but something beyond her control drew her to a spot behind the tavern not far from the mass grave. Almost completely hidden in the earth and grass was a comer of a stone marker, sticking out. From a distance she thought that it might have been another Gestapo man following her but soon she saw the white cane extended before him. As they stood above the spot where the white fence had guarded Chayele's grave, she tried to speak.

"This, Josef, is the first grave, the first Jewish grave in Watermill. It would have been strange indeed for anyone to see the town Madame and the blind German colonel standing in the field behind the tavern on such a miserable day. As they walked away, he told her of Jod'l's call.

XIII

Lieutanant Erich von Schmidt lay back on his chaise, relaxed. He still thought of himself as a lieutenant even though he had been honorably promoted to Kolonel in the Intelligence Korps. All the big shots were there, Himmler, Heydrich, Eichmann and the Feuhrer. It was too impressive. The pity was that he couldn't see them. His recovery from the blast in the laboratory was complete and if not for his loss of sight, he would be perfect. He couldn't read any of the books that he loved. He couldn't enjoy the art that he loved, the art the Reich had rescued from the galleries that they had conquered. He couldn't see the large original posters of the Feurer that he had secured at great cost and cunning. At least he could listen to the phonograph and his collection of Telefunken recordings of the Berlin Symphony, The Berlin National Opera. Who could compare to Wagner, the trumpets blaring the "Ride of the Valkyrie," as he beat the air in front of him to the rhythm of the music? What could compare to the rising crescendo, to the victory? The official army band had played that music, Hitler's favorite, when they hung the Iron Cross around his neck barely a week after his release from the military hospital. Over and over the phonograph blared the theme. It was funny, he thought now that he was blind, how more vividly he could see the charge, Die Helden, the heroes. His heart swelled with German pride until he was reminded of his blindness. The record ended with the repeated click of the needle in the end track. He leaned over and felt his way to remove the tone arm but someone beat him to it. The music was so loud that he hadn't heard anyone approach.

"Erich mein liebe!" It was his girlfriend's soft voice. "Erich! There was a call from headquarters." He didn't interrupt her but his mind said, "What could they want with me? They had made me a Kolonel and now they were going to discharge me?

Now that I'm useless." He rose to his full six feet, a magnificent specimen of the Master Race, a blond, blue-eyed hero now relegated to a cripple. Marta interrupted his silent tirade. "They want you to report to the unit for briefing. Something to do with Polish insurgents."

He sat back down in the chaise looking up at her. "Poland? What the hell do I know about Poland?"

She calmly answered, "Perhaps after the briefing you'll be an expert. Anyway, it beats sitting here listening to Wagner. The appointment is for tomorrow, so we must get ready!" Her demeanor seemed to change as she gave him the order to get going. He had to change and assume his role as an Intelligence Officer, even if it was only in Poland. Herr Kolonel von Schmidt would be ready. The briefing took six whole days. Marta returned home while he was billeted at headquarters. His orders were cut, he was assigned a driver and a Volkswagen motor car equipped with bullet-proofing and two bright Nazi flags that would flap vigorously as the vehicle sped to his new assignment. If it was the beat of the motor or flapping flags he couldn't tell but it enhanced the "Ride of the Valkyrie" that kept blaring in his head and burst from his lusty throat. "Da de de da da . . ." He was on his way! It was driving the driver crazy but he said nothing. He wished it would stop and when it occasionally did he was grateful. Then it started again, Erich couldn't control himself. The map that the driver was to follow was pretty simple. The Autobahn was perfect; even the main roads in Poland were good. It appeared that the Poles were accepting, if not hospitable. If it was not a military establishment where they stayed for food and lodging, he always paid generously. He was polite and handsome and even in his officer's uniform, the local people extended him courtesy. Perhaps because he was blind.

How the secret of this trip had leaked out or by whom, no one ever knew. Even the young Russian lieutenant and his assistant did not know more than the information that the blind German colonel was going to leave for Pilski exactly at 7 A.M., Tuesday morning. The trap was set and the colonel's car would have to stop to change the flat tires. Josef Slomovitch almost felt guilty taking advantage of this helpless man, but he was the enemy and the job had to be done. The Soviet command had invested time and money to prepare him for this job. His country depended on him. The Volkswagon appeared on the horizon, its dust plume signaling its arrival. Blam! The driver reacted quickly to control the vehicle. The blind colonel had been thrown over but he soon regained his composure, got out of the car and found a grassy knoll to sit down on. He encouraged the driver to hurry, not being aware of his six-foot blond, blue-eyed replica who was about to end his trip, forever. The Russian lieutenant's driver finished replacing the flattened tires and set about burying the two Germans who would no longer be of service to the Third Reich. The vehicle that they had arrived in also had to be destroyed so that no evidence could ever be found. All of the clothes he would no longer need were neatly packed in the Kolonel's bags as well as the other necessities. Soon they would be ready to continue on to the city of Pilski and then on to Watermill. The dark glasses in place, his prepared identification, his uniform, everything had to be perfect for the plan to work. He was now Erich von Schmidt, colonel in the great German Wehrmacht. As they reached the top of the hill he asked the driver to tell him what he saw ahead. The driver said he saw a castle the likes of which he had never seen.

XIV

Maryushka didn't have time on her side. She practically ran to the church. The father, half asleep, invited her in. She outlined the plan and he agreed to do his part. The pilgrimage would begin at sunrise. No sooner did she thank him she ran to the houses where the girls were waiting. It was a bright moonlit night so she needed no illumination. One by one she alerted the girls to be ready at first light to leave for Pilski. "Wear simple clothing, carry the rosary in your hand but take as much jewelry as you can hide!" she advised them. The father would meet them at the church, where army trucks would take them to the city. She sternly cautioned them not to speak to anyone. She entered her house and held her elecric torch under her blanket, where she scribbled one word, "EVACUATE!" Again she was out in the eerie moonlight, heading toward the tavern. She knocked two times, then three more and waited. The door opened slightly to show the barkeep in his nightshirt. He held his fingers to his lips, pleading silence. The paper in her outstreched hand was snatched away and the door shut. "G-d, I hope he reads the message," she thought. "I hope he understands it and spreads the word." There was no time to lose. What had she seen? Was it two Gestapo men lying drunk on the tavern floor or were they dead or was it an illusion created by the moonlight?

She went back to her house but could not sleep. The adrenaline running through her veins gave her a headache. She had to prepare a picnic basket with kilbasa, fruit and wine and a loaf of Polish black bread. Underneath it she hid the Luger that one of the girls had stolen. It was loaded and ready. Over it all she placed a beautifully embroided Polish babushka. Everything was ready. Despite her effort, she nodded off until the screeching of the crows as they took flight from the Schloss tower woke her. Her clock read five-thirty. She looked out the window and saw the girls, like shadows float across the fields on their way to the church. She saw the barkeep slip out of the tavern with the warning message in his hand headed to the partisans. The two Gestapo men on the floor lay there in a sleep from which they would never awaken.

The sun was skimming over the mountains, its rays spreading out like a halo, bringing in a new beautiful day. Watermill lay still and idyllic in its valley. Soon it would be a ghost town except for the Germans. The people had seen the slaughter of the Jews, why wait for the same fate? An orderly had gassed up the officer's car for the colonel. He and Fritz were going for a picnic in the woods. "A beautiful lady would join them," he explained as the orderly parked the car outside the gate of the Shloss. And just as he said, the beautiful Maryushka approached the parked vehicle with the picnic basket and took her seat on the passenger's side. The orderly walked away without saluting the colonel; because he knew the officer couldn't see. Only Helga, standing in the doorway of the Shloss, noticed that Erich had approached the car, with the Madame, threw his cane into the back seat beside Fritz, got in behind the wheel and drove away.

Epilogue

ACCORDING TO SCHEDULE, the S.S.Gestapo, with reinforcements from the barracks in Pilski, swooped down on Watermill with a vengeance. They found the two Gestapo men in the tavern. The Grupen Feurer was livid. "Everyone must die! Everyone!" Those were his orders. When he was told that no one was to be found his rage was unimaginable. He swore that he would personally hunt down every one of these Polish swine. If it wasn't planned before, it would be now. "Burn the place down!" he ordered and the Black and Skulls set everything afire. The thick smoke rose, enveloping the town. The dry summer wind set the straw and grass on fire surrounding the Gestapo men, setting their uniforms on fire. As they ran around screaming, running away from the firestorm, the crows from the castle flew over them, screeching agitated from the smoke.

All was gone in smoldering embers, all except the Shloss and Magistrate. Ironically some of the sparks had set the swastika banners that had adorned the walls of the castle on fire. Only a memorial plaque remains on the heavy oak door of the Shloss, a national shrine, to mark where the town of Watermill once stood.

Maryushka escaped to the east because of the documents Slomovitch had prepared and his uniform was respected by the Germans until he reached the Red army. Once he declared his true identity, he was received as a hero and returned to his wife and children in the interior of the Soviet Union, where he continued to serve until the end of hostilities.

Return Home

III

Preface

THE WAR WAS over and the chaos that came with it was now replaced with a new chaos, fraught with new corruption and a new recrimination. The hopes of rebirth would be replaced by problems unforeseen. For Maryushka and Josef, the future would become enmeshed in situations which they had never planned and in which they had no desire to get involved.

EM

Acknowledgement: Much of the true history I gleaned from my beloved parents and relatives who survived the Shoah!

Return Home

I

THE WAR WAS over. That Slomovitch's contribution was significant was evident in the medals he was awarded. Everybody in Russia was awarded medals but his were unusual. Not everyone had the "Special Services Award," the "Hero of the Soviet Union," or the coveted "Order of Lenin" medal. Although he returned to his position at the University and wore the medals with pride on his academic robes, he still had a strange longing for the idyllic Watermill. His wife and children had weathered the terrible life of the war years and now were living through the post-war period. But the war had taken its toll on his wife's health. The fact that they were the family of an important celebrity was certainly helpful in the bureaucratic system. Josef, after all, was a highly decorated Russian officer and had been rewarded for his extraordinary service to the motherland with a promotion to the rank of vice-marshal. Actually, the promotion was honorary because it came upon retirement from the Red Army. It paid off in his status and pension. Nothing in the record indicated that he was a Jew. As far as the government was concerned, neither heroes in the army or resistance were ever recorded by their ethnicity, for all were "Comrades of the Soviet Union."

The histories of the 'War Against Fascism' made no mention either of the small towns or villages that made the supreme sacrifices and suffered destruction at the hand of the German Wehrmacht and Gestapo. This bothered him very much. Anything about Poland was omitted, so the episode of the Pilski Bridge or the Town of Watermill was never recorded. At first, he saw this as an oversight. However, in truth, it was the major cities that had played the decisive role in the defeat of the enemy. As time went on, the omission by the historians began to bother him more. It did not disturb him that his spy mission was never included because that was a clandestine operation, but he felt that the omission of the heroic contribution of people like Maryushka, the priest and the girls of Watermill, was unfair. He was concerned that the many Watermills throughout the region, the heroic, patriotic people who played a role in helping to defeat the enemy, would be lost to posterity.

Their arrival in Moscow had given Josef the opportunity to continue his work in military intelligence, at the top echelons. What about Miriam? Upon her reaching Moscow, she immediately enlisted as a nurse and was given a post in a military hospital. Her skills as a nurse and leader soon became evident and the job of superintendant at a field unit was offered to her. The casualties were so many that nurses had to do double duty, as nurses and doctors. Josef's success in MI earned him recognition from Marshal Voroshilov. When hostilities ended, Miriam continued on in her nursing job but she longed to return home. The letters that she sent were returned undeliverable at first. Then they began to get through. She heard from the priest that the devastation that the fire had caused was being addressed. Slow progress was taking place. After all, Watermill was a low priority on any list. What did have priority was convening the Court of Justice, where collaborators were being judged and punished. Oddly enough, the witnesses who came forward against the others in these courts were often collaborators themselves. When Miriam found out that her girls were in jeopardy, she terminated her stay in the Soviet Union. The Court had already judged many cases when the girls were charged with consorting with the enemy. The priest had been on the stand for days as the prosecutor kept questioning him. No matter what the father said, his explanation was defied. The prosecutor sneered, "Reverend Father, do you deny or affirm that you had relations with these women?"

"Yes! As their confessor. Indeed I did."

"All we need is a simple 'Yes' or 'No!'" After a pause he continued. "Your Eminence," the prosecutor asked sarcastically, "Tell the People's Court, did you or did you not minister to enemy soldiers in your church?"

"Yes, I did, as I did to all Catholics, as I did to members of my own flock!" he replied. He had heard of many clergymen who were being convicted as collaborators. He knew some priests who were guilty. He had to tell the truth but he also had to keep his oath of silence as a confessor and about the Underground operation.

"What role did you and these women play, as it is rumored, in counter-enemy activities?"

The father looked toward the women in the dock and back at the inquisitor. "My oath prohibits me from answering."

"Therefore the accusations against all these women as traitors stands as against that they were patriots! No further questions!" He addressed the Court. "This witness will be dealt with subsequently!"

Just as the father stepped down, a noise came from the corridor as the police guards tried to keep the woman from entering the courtroom in the Magistrate. The gavel cracked the Courtroom into silence. The stately figure wearing the nurse's uniform of the Red Army marched right up to the bench. "Your grace!" her voice rang strong and authoritarian through the court. "If anyone should be on trial, it is I! I am the Madame! My name is Maryushka!"

The courtroom became chaos. Cameras flashed, voices murmured. The presiding judge called for order and adjourned over the objections of the prosecutor. Everyone filed out of the old courtroom except the Madame, her girls and the priest. One by one Maryushka hugged them. There were plenty of tears, tears of joy, tears of sorrow, sorrow at the crazy turn of events that was taking place.

II

The following morning, the courthouse was full and the crowds overflowed onto the steps. Not everyone knew Maryushka personally, because she had business in the Jew section of town, but even those who had known her were ready to condemn her off hand. This day she was wearing a simple skirt and a blouse beautifully embroidered in the Polish style. Her graying blond hair was put up in braids crowning her head and she had on a minimum of makeup. The girls sat apprehensively in the dock, the priest in the public section. There was a noticeable distance between the father and the people near him. The call to order came and the clerk called Maryushka alias Miriam Aragon to the witness stand. She stood and gracefully entered the box, then took her seat after taking the oath. It was obvious that the bible the pre-war regime used in the court had been dispensed with.

"If it pleases the court, I ask your indulgence for one minute. There is a matter of great urgency to bring to your attention. We have evidence that his Excellency, Mr. Prosecutor, alias Tadiuski, alias "FOX," was instrumental in the capture and execution of "Black Crow!" We have proof that the leader of our guerilla unit was betrayed to the Gestapo by FOX. The evidence will show the prosecutor's anti-Semitic hatred led him to help the enemy trap Black Crow, our most revered leader, who was Jewish." This news shocked the courtroom. Over his protests, the prosecutor was immediately arrested and taken to jail. The case against FOX would come soon enough, but for the moment the charges against Miriam, the priest and the girls needed to be disposed of. Then a new prosecutor would be found and the evidence amassed for the most renowned trial of all, the murder of Black Crow! It had been a terrible blow to the people's war. The news of what was happening in Watermill became a national and international story. Maryushka's picture was plastered all over the press. She was very happy and surprised to get a telephone call from Josef. What could she say? "Acquitted?"

III

That the People's Court had concluded that they all were innocent would be a miracle in itself When the court heard each of the girls' testimony, they found it incredible. Even the corroborative statements of the priest and Maryushka were not convincing enough. Were they not co-conspirators after all? They were up against the whole town's opinion that they indeed collaborated and consorted. It had been obvious! Those who knew that it was through Miriam and the priest that they were saved from the massacre by the Gestapo remained silent for fear of recrimination. The only other witness who could be of help was silent. The old Shloss just stood there, silently, a silent witness. It's cold stone walls seared by the Nazi's flames could not bear witness in court. An examination of Slomovitch's quarters held nothing to support their story. Even the black crows were silent as they flew out of their perches, as a result of the acrid smoke of the Gestapo's fire. Except for the Magistrat and a few of the official buildings that the fire could not destroy, only the Shloss remained unscathed. When the people returned it became the temporary governmental headquarters until the Magistrate was rehabilitated. The heavy stone walls had protected whatever the Germans left behind. Josef's quarters were left intact, for it would have been more trouble to remove the things than it was worth. But the room gave no proof to support Maryushka's story. Only the piece of paper from Slomovitch had saved them. The case against them was not settled until his letter arrived. His chronology was precise. His proof indisputable! The seal authoritative. Result? Acquitted!

Now it was time to go on. Maryushka took a long walk around her beloved town. How bleak her Watermill was, even though the seared grass was beginning to let new growth appear. She visited the plot where a small marble stone still marked the first Jewish grave and she wiped the char from it. The name "Chayele," was barely legible now. She gazed over the flattening mound of the mass grave the Nazis had left behind. She caught her tears as they ran down her cheeks. What would be her future, now that she returned to Watermill?

Her Watermill had to be rebuilt. Priority number one, housing. Another winter in makeshift hovels would be devastating. When she approached the mayor, he laughed at her. "Daughter," he said, "there are priorities and there are priorities! In this district, Pilski rates above us and the other villages. It is, after all, the seat of government and power. Now that the bridge has been repaired, the heavy building equipment can get through. Our poor roads cannot carry such traffic. First we need a road, then buildings!" Before she could argue the point, he rose to dismiss her. "You're a nurse! We need a hospital." "What hospital?" she cried. "That shack you call a hospital? There will be a greater need for a hospital if we don't get housing before winter!" He ended, "I'm glad the case against you, the priest and the girls was dropped. Keep me advised about how things work out! Road, then buildings!" Before she could argue the point, he dismissed her. "You're a nurse; good day!"

She didn't move.

"It is over my head! Go to Pilski! See if you can get somewhere with them. After all, you and your priest and your whores have become national heroes!" He stalked out of the office, leaving Maryushka alone. She stood there for what seemed a long time. Was it frustration or bigotry that was expressed. She would give the mayor the benefit of the doubt.

IV

Finding the Pilski City Hall was no simple task. Maryushka made her way from the railroad station through the confusion of the mass construction. The old City Hall seemed dwarfed among all the giant structures going up around it. At the information desk she was directed to an office on the second floor. She entered the office with the words, "District Construction Commissar." The secretary advised her that there were many appointments and that she had to wait. When it appeared that she might have to return the next day, she demanded an audience. She insisted that she represented the town of Watermill. When she suggested that a trip to Warsaw might get her needs addessed, the door to the inner office opened.

"Your Grace!" she began as she pushed her way into the office.

"No! No!" he interrupted. "We don't use those words, anymore. Where are you from?"

Maryushka introduced herself, then reminded the commissar how the guerrilla unit from Watermill stopped the Germans cold on the bridge in Pilski. A broad smile crossed his face as she kept pushing her case. "We recognize the urgency for reconstructing the city, but all we need in Watermill is a better road."

"Is that all?" he whispered "By the way, your unit was not alone. I was there, too. However, you know it's not so easy to get this damn bureaucracy moving, no less than change something!"

She had not come this far for nothing but consolation. "I don't want to have to go to Warsaw to complain, but it is a matter of life and death. I am a nurse and my credentials in the Red Army speaks for themselves. Watermill needs a wider road for construction trucks to get through and build housing before the winter weather. We don't need theaters and museums. We need homes and a hospital. If you could face the danger of the Germans, if you could blow up a bridge, you could do this!"

She stopped, emotionally drained. The commissar said nothing but began writing. She could not tell what he was writing. Then he suddenly stopped. "All right! You can go home!" That was all. In his mind, he kept hearing, "road, homes, hospital, BUDGET!" In her mind she heard, "Go home!"

The trip back to Watermill was long and uncomfortable. Transportation from Pilski was never good but the discomfort was exacerbated by the uncertainty that she left with. No commitment was made and no assurance that her interview made any difference. She would return with nothing to tell her people and the fear of failure bothered her deeply. It took several days for her to get up the courage to write Josef. Little did she realize that he was having his own problems. Her Poland and his Russia were going through the same rebirth. In his simple reply, he wrote that he hoped that the Polish construction engineers were better than those in his country. Many faults in the system that had resulted in waste and danger were being covered up by the bureaucracy. They frowned on a University professor butting into their business. Years ago, the

KGB censors would have removed such comments from his letters, but they were too busy with other matters to bother. His letters were fine but not good enough.

She needed to talk to someone and that someone was Josef. Getting to him on the phone was a big hassle but once she heard his voice, everything seemed less problematic. He said that he was certain that his phone was being bugged but he didn't care.

"My concern is with my boys in college. They had been in the Red Youth Komsomol since they were kids but they were encountering anti-Zionist anti-Semitic pressure from peers at school. Even with the death of Stalin and the reporting of the purges, I thought that problem would have abated. Well, I guess you have the same thing in Poland." Josef neglected to mention that his wife was in the hospital, in critical condition. He knew that Maryushka would return to Moscow, to help, if she knew.

She answered, "I've heard of some terrible happenings in Russia but here in Watermill there are far worse things for the population to worry about. If the government doesn't get busy with housing, it will be catastrophic." The conversation continued with them both feeling better.

V

The sign on the door to his office read, "Josef Slomovitch, Prof." but it was hard to read because the door was seldom closed. Among other things, his open-door policy made "Professor Joe" very popular on campus. This morning, two figures stood in his doorway and they were neither students. Without knocking, one asked, "Slomovitch?"

His reply was a simple, "Da!" His gut feeling that this was no social call, otherwise they would have made an appointment. The two chairs that were against the wall were repositioned and the men sat down across the desk from him. There was no conversation at first. Josef simply waited as the men sucked in the information that the walls with his credentials could provide. One then took out a pipe and proceeded to light it, sending plumes of acrid smoke into his immaculate office. He had to stifle a cough. Never in all his training and years in Intelligence had he seen such a charade. As though a signal was given, the pipe stem was pointed at him and a gravelly voice behind it began.

"Honorable Professor. We are from the . . ." He need not have explained, Josef thought. How could they out fox a fox? The talk droned on in which all the data in Josef's dossier was acknowledged. His whole life, parents, school, membership in the right organizations, his military career, his marriage, children, etc. He wished they would get to the point. Finally, the smoker stopped to puff and blow. Josef rose and went to open the window. He hoped the smoker would get the hint, but it didn't work. Was this a new chemical the KGB had invented to make one tell the truth?

"Solomovitch!" the other began. If the situation were not so solemn, Josef might have laughed. This man's voice was high pitched. almost feminine and the contrast was absolutely comical.

"We know that your record and your patriotism are unquestionable. Your wife's record is impeccable as well. However, we have some unfortunate; let us say disturbing, information regarding one of your sons. Are you aware of his affiliation with anti-Soviet elements?"

Actually, Slomovitch had little knowledge of what his sons were doing. They were grown men, in college and he was busy with his work and with his wife. He remained silent but his mind was screaming. The stench from the pipe was becoming nauseating. He had been a pipe smoker for years but this garbage was becoming intolerable. Where was all the good

Cuban tobacco? He gestured with his hand several times but the pipe kept belching its smoke. “Do you mind?” waving his hand again, to disperse the fumes. Apparently, smoker must have become deaf and blind from the smoke.

The Castrato, non-smoker, took out a pad began to write. “Is that your reply?” he said.

“Is that your reply to what?” Josef answered seriously.

“Professor, this is serious. This is not a time to be coy!” he shot back, his voice going higher. “We don’t want to have you down as uncooperative!”

At this, Josef became upset. “Gentlemen, my time is valuable. I put up with your intrusion, your stinking up my office, your insinuation and now your threat. When you have something to offer other than a stinking herring, I’ll be happy to be cooperative. Until then, as they say in French, ‘Auf Wiedersehn!’” He stood up gesturing the two men to the door, “. . . and put the chairs where you found them!” Then, “My complaint to your superiors will be immediate if not sooner!”

Deja-vu! Hadn’t he used those words when he was a German officer in the Shloss in Watermill. Sure! He would complain. “The agents, no name! One a gravel-voiced smoker, the other a soprano!” He couldn’t stop a smile from replacing the anger he felt. Now to make the call.

Dmitri answered the phone on the seventh ring. “Oh! It’s you, Dad!” his voice showing surprise. Is it Mom?” For most of their lives, this war and all, the Slomovitch boys had little contact with their father. Sure, they were proud of him but he had been a virtual stranger. As teenagers, they had suspicions about their father’s fidelity, with all the talk of the nurse from Poland.

“Dimmy!” Josef still called him by his nickname. “Let’s get together, tonight. We can visit Mother, then go to dinner. Can you get in touch with your brother? I don’t have his new number.” There was a pause. “Dmitri! Are you there?”

“Yes! Father. Is it important?

"What do you mean important? Your mother or dinner with me?"

"Father!" That tone of voice! That awful feeling that it evoked in Slomovitch.

Then, "Well, OK. What time? At the campus café?"

"Well, no! Let's meet at the hospital. Say, seven. I'll reserve a parking space for you, then we can decide. You'll call Anatole!" There was no reply, just the click of a hang-up. Josef held the receiver to his ear a long time, unable to return it to its cradle. Were his children insensitive, callous, or just mean. Had the system removed familial love from the psyche or had the state really succeeded in replacing the family. The noise signaled for him to return the receiver.

VI

Maryushka told no one but her closest friends about her trip to Pilski. Actually, she was embarrased at having failed in her mission. She thought that had she been a man, an engineer, a Party operative with clout, things would have turned out differently. Early Monday morning, the sun shone bright and clear but Watermill was being shaken by a thunderous noise. From the hill, far behind the Shloss, an immense cloud of dust parted to expose a convoy of gigantic road-building equipment. Everyone came out to cheer and welcome this miracle. At that time no one knew who was responsible. Everyone assumed it was the Mayor or some big shot in the government.

Because the road was too narrow, the foreman in the lead truck stopped the convoy and asked who was in charge. The Mayor strode forward, as proud as a peacock. The foreman held an order sheet toward the Mayor and said, "I need someone called 'Maryushka!'"

BBBut, I'm the Mayor. he sputtered. To one of his aides he whispered, "Get the Jew nurse! Hurry!"

When she arrived, she was met with a big hurrah. The foreman greeted her as an old acquaintance. Miriam invited all the crewmen to have tea. She told the foreman to show her the plans for the improved roadway. Together they went over the route. Maryushka realized that what she saw was very bad. No one had consulted anyone in Watermill. What was being proposed would violate all the land that for generations had been held sacrosanct. Her joy now was turned into misery. It called for drastic action. She had to hold up the construction in any way possible. It would take much too long for a return to Pilski. The foreman was adamant. He had his orders and nothing was going to stop him. Nothing!

Well, Mr. Nothing was busy in Pilski. When the commissar got on the phone, he expected all kinds of gratitude but what he got from Maryushka was not joyful. Of course she thanked him. Then came the BUT!

He was absolutely correct. His engineers had done an excellent and efficient job. None of the maps showed any gravesites. Perhaps the excavators could move the graves to a better location. Sure he recognized the historic significance but any detour would make the project too expensive and an on-site survey would take months to get approved. Maryushka felt that the other landmarks had been overlooked as well, but she realized that the engineers had no way of knowing the emotional attachment the people had to the special place in town as it used to be. In spite of her nostalgia she realized that any restructuring would omit the Jewish quarter with the shops, the tailor's, the blacksmith, the hardware store, the very first business to settle in Watermill, and the tavern where the locals could find comfort in the homemade shlivovitz or fruit flavored shnapps. How could they know or care about the old synagogue that had stood for generations, then was burned to the ground with the congregation inside? Even the old church that remained, though the cathedral had been built to replace it. The church that had been used to hide the cache of weapons and members of the Underground or fugitives hiding from the Gestapo. That was all in the not-so-long ago that seemed like ages ago. A few Jews had returned to Watermill after the war. Most who had survived had fled to the west to be relocated to Israel, America, Canada or South America. For many, the memories of their suffering, the loss of family and friends in the camps was much too hard to return to. That too many Polish nationals had actually sympathized with the Nazis in their hatred of the Jews was evident. Some had been guilty of massacring Jews who had returned to reclaim their old home and property after the war. These incidents discouraged others.

When Josef had asked her why she had decided to return to Watermill, Maryushka explained, "It is my duty! Someone has to protect the memory of what Watermill was before the war, during the war. If not me, who? If not now? When?" He couldn't understand why she had begun to laugh. "Haven't you ever heard of Hillel?" She cried and then proceeded to explain. It seems that she was right! Were she not there to testify at the trial, her friends would have been crucified. The Shloss had witnessed it all but could say nothing.

Now, with the struggle she had with the road construction and the Pilski commissar, she realized how right she was. She tried to be discreet as possible, not to embarrass either of these men publically, but her argument won out and she was invited to renegotiate the route of the new roadway. The idea of a great memorial park on the site of the massacre that would honor the Polish heroes in the war was considered a stroke of genius. Of course the commissar was to get the credit. As usual, Maryushka'a tenacity and brains had won out. She knew it and the people knew it.

The roadway problem was settled but the prospect of a memorial park on such prime property was not acceptable to the town council. She found many who turned a deaf ear to her pleas. Many who were on the council witnessed the massacre and were silent. Some had even helped the Nazis round up the Jews and even turned in their rescuers. She had to win them over, not alienate them. Their plans would have a huge housing development exactly where the park site was to be. Her victory with the construction commissar was being overturned. There were so many reasons for their intransigence. Bureaucrats could be persuaded, even bribed. Not with money but with deals.

The toughest council members were the old guard, the anti-Semitic Catholics on the one hand and the fanatic Communists on the other. Maryushka wasn't sure that these men had ever heard of Josef Slomovitch or his heroism. At the meeting to discuss the conflict, she secretly arranged a speaker-phone. When she mentioned having a hero of the Red Army on the line, there were shouts of disapproval. But no sooner had Josef's voice come on than they settled down to listen. "Comrades! Brothers! Councilmen! The pure Polish words hit home. He went on briefly to identify himself, his civilian position, his military rank. Then his friendly tone changed. "Gentlemen! It would be a disgrace to the honor of the gallant Polish people, the Polish Army, the Polish Resistance for you to allow this final resting place of all those Polish citizens, Jewish and non-Jewish, to be desecrated. There lie the remains of Polish victims, the blood of innocent Polish men, women and children slaughtered before your very eyes with German machineguns. Are you going to dispose of these victims of the war against Fascism as though they were a dung heap?" Here his voice again became conciliatory. "As a brother, I know that you will do honor to those who have made Watermill soil holy!"

Silence! Josef had signed off Maryushka's face was flooded with tears. She turned away, embarrassed. The Mayor began so softly that his voice was hardly audible.

"My child, what you have done deserves the highest praise and we thank you! We have suffered so much death and loss that in our zeal to rebuild, we sometimes forget those whom we lost. Tomorrow, we will discuss the matter, which I believe will be agreed upon. In that case we would be honored to have you on the memorial park committee to help us design it appropriately!"

Maryushka was too moved to say anything. She was amazed that she had prevailed again. The improved roadway was completed sooner than realized and vast materials were being stockpiled for the rebuilding of Watermill. Maryushka was asked to approve the plans and she was delighted to be of help. This in addition to her work at the hospital and her pet project, the construction of a modern hospital. The sound of building around her was music to her ears. What set all of this into motion, she wasn't sure, but if she was responsible somehow, she never crowed about it.

One day, her telephone rang with a call from Pilski. She thought it might have been the construction commissar but it was someone she didn't know. The man at the other end began with polite chatter, asking after her health, how Watermill was getting on, etc. She made an effort to satisfy the questions but was anxious to have the voice get to the point. He never identified himself by name or office. Finally, he got to the point.

"Sister Maryushka, I am in charge of the Central Library in Pilski and we are trying to amass a record of the pertinent material regarding the history of our region, before and during the war. Your name has come to our office as someone who could do a magnificent job in this role." She could hear the wheezing breath at the other end. Before she could answer, he said, "We have sufficient funds!" Another wheezing pause, then, "You're the only one we can trust!"

VII

The Pilski librarian said that he would put everything into action. Maryushka had to decide whether she would undertake such an important task, which was very difficult to accept, considering all of her other commitments, but given the gravity of the assignment, she could hardly refuse.

She was given sufficient time to arrange for replacement at the hospital. Funds were supplied for some minimal staff, many of which were college students who were eager to earn credit in the humanities. The work was very tedious and at times menial but she was able to establish a collection of fine works by Polish poets and authors. Many religious books that had been hidden and saved needed to be found and reconditioned. There would be a room in the library kept as a museum. Artifacts left by the Holocaust victims would have a special section. Maryushka made a personal call to Moscow. "Josef! You wouldn't believe what happened!" He was happy for her. "Whatever I can do to help, let me know! Why don't you check out the Shloss? After all that's the oldest structure in Watermill! The crypt might have some unique treasure. By the way, you might take some of the junk from my room in the tower as a sample of wartime history." he chuckled.

Maryushka told him about the fight she had when the roadway detour was approved with his help. She mentioned the possibility of the creation of the memorial park. She didn't go into details that had her ending up pleading her case to the Warsaw authorities. How the housing construction that was planned would have replaced the park which she had fought for. She also never mentioned that she planned to get his help if everything failed. Fortunately, that wasn't necessary. They talked about the boys and his wife's condition. The call ended with cheerful best wishes in spite of the difficulties both were facing. She rang off. She completely forgot to tell him about the proposal that she head up the library project. Well, that hadn't happened yet and she wasn't the only one holding back reporting their problems.

Slomovitch, being a professor in a prestigious university in Moscow, had kept away from the controversial turmoil that was swirling around him. Not exactly oblivious but not involved. It was therefore troubling that the visit from the KGB should have come to his doorstep. He had been a tacit member of the right organizations, played the role of the patriot and done his duty. His children had been thoroughly indoctrinated and grown up in the Communist youth organizations. But they were grown men. The world had changed. Zionism was looked upon as a threat to the Soviet Union, who sided with the Arab countries shortly after they supported recognition of Israel. The opportunity for anti-Semitism was again overtly excusable. That the name Slomovitch was not ethnically Russian was cause for concern. His parents were virtually non-Jewish. The old generation of practicing orthodoxy was long gone or indeed a non-entity. The government's efforts to eradicate Jewishness had succeeded for many years, or so it seemed. With the end of Stalinism it was thought that greater freedom of religion would be realized, but that was not achieved. The KGB was infiltrating the organizations that were winning interest of the young people who were of Jewish descent. The Lubovitch Rebbe was sending men and religious articles for the returnees to Judaism. Their organization was called the Jewish Resurgence Movement.

VIII

Seven o'clock! Two fine looking young men got out of the car and made their way from the parking area toward the Oncology building. There would be no joy in seeing their mother; the agony of her terminal cancer had been going on for over a year. Josef knew this would be the last time that she would be able to respond, even so weakly, to them. The orderly advised them to limit their visit. Josef took her hand, cold and limp. Her eyes remained closed. They never would know whether it was on purpose or not. Nothing could be said. The boys merely stood at the bedside, also mute. Soon they left. There seemed to be no attachment between them and the person in the bed. The cafeteria in the hospital basement was practically empty. Josef led the way to a corner table. He scanned the walls for any secreted cameras or microphones. No place was not suspect. The music background might have helped but modem surveillance techniques were beyond comprehension. The boys went to the counter for food. The hospital fare was simple but their purpose was not dining out. Nothing was said for some time, then Josef tried to begin.

"Dmitri, Anatole . . . please allow me to explain. Mother is gone! Do you care to be at her funeral?" There was a pause, then the older son nodded, the younger followed his lead. "I really have some important questions," Josef began.

"And we have some of our own," Dmitri answered. His cold demeanor was apparent.

"Which first? Slomovitch replied. "O.K. You first."

"Who is this woman Marushka? You never talk about her, yet you seem to be very tight with her! Of course you don't have to . . ."

Josef was taken aback and took a little time to arrange his thought. The sons thought he was not about to confide to them his illicit relationship. Then he began. "I don't have to tell you all the details of my experience in Watermill, much of which you know, but one thing be assured, Miriam or Maryushka as you know her, and I had no romantic connection. Not that it wasn't tempting on both our parts. Trust me, our job and our survival were our uttermost concern. Nothing else!" As he spoke he looked directly into their eyes. The pain of such a question he kept deep down inside himself where he kept the secret liaison with Helga. "Thanks to Maryushka our victory over the Germans was greatly hastened. It was through her that our family in Watermill was revealed after all these years. The mystery of the Shloss and our ancestors who came to Russia years ago. No! No relationship!" None of them had touched their food all the time that he was speaking. Now they were too moved to eat.

Anatole was the first to speak. "What was your question, Papa?" Josef hadn't heard that word in too long a time. How he would treasure this moment.

"Let's eat!" he suggested. They all dug in, their hunger quite apparent. After the dessert and coffee he got to the point of this visit. "You wouldn't believe the visit I had from the 'B!'" The derisive term for the KGB. He went on to describe the two clowns that had come to his office. They were hysterical the way Josef mimicked the men, Smoker and Castrato. They hadn't had such fun together since before the war when they were kids. Would this reunite the family again? But there was the question: "What have you been up to, to warrant the KGB warning?"

Anatole deferred to his brother. Dmitri hesitated but began by explaining about the assaults that were coming from the other students. This led to their seeking out the JRM. The professor had heard of the Jewish Resurgence Movement but had never thought to investigate it. He certainly was not interested in Zionism or Judaism as a religion, even though he realized that he was an ethnic Jew by birth, whatever that meant. First and foremost, he was a Soviet citizen! But all these thoughts had to be shunted aside so that they wouldn't interfere with Dimmy's talk.

"We were skeptical to say the least. At least I was! The guys that approached me were a little wierd, to say the least. They wanted to be different, separate. They flaunted their newfound connection to old world religion. But they were not nut cases.

They were the cream of academia. Many are students of yours. That's why they approached me." Here he paused, waiting to see what reaction he was getting from his father. Josef's nod signaled him to continue. Actually, Anatole had a different approach. He set out to investigate. There had been a secret group of Lubovitch followers who held Minyan every day at a home off campus. When he was approached by one of them, he did not want to get involved but the pressure of the anti-Zionists made him change his mind. The Lubovitcher did not claim to be Zionist in the contemporary sense.

Anatole tried to explain. "The men that I found there were not political at all. What they wanted was to bring the Jewish students back to their heritage, their roots, their religion. I felt strange at first but then I realized that I was really not a Russian. My name, though Russianized, wasn't Russian either. When they opened the bible and instead of Anatole, they found the name Abraham and then Aaron, I got a strange feeling. Had I actually been named for one of those ancestors? It seemed that I was drawn to this place, these people. By accident, or was it ordained? Then I met my brother there." Again the two boys were examining their father's eyes for his reaction. Josef said nothing. He stroked his chin as though there were whiskers there. Both boys began to laugh, "That's what the Rabbi does to the beard on his chin."

"It must be generic!" smiled Josef. "I often find myself doing things I can't explain."

The food was finished, even the extra cup of coffee, but the conversation continued. In the back of his mind, Slomovitch kept asking himself, "What have I missed all these years?" But the problem wasn't them; it was the KGB! So he turned the question back to that ominous-humorous visit. "Why do you think the 'B' visited me after all these years?"

It was Dmitri's turn to explain. "Maybe it would be better if we took a walk!" They rose and made their way out, when

Dimmy insisted on paying the check, Josef was pleasantly surprised. It was a mild day as they made their way to Gorky Park, famously known for the clandestine assignations. The idea crossed each of their minds but nothing was said. What a day this had been so far. The sorrow, the joy, seemed to mix in a strange way. The KGB, his dying wife, the meeting, their new orientation! Strange indeed! And now they were strolling side by side into Gorky. The professor stopped at a secluded bench and motioned for them to sit down but the boys opted to stand. Josef sat, his years showing, happy for the chance to get off his feet. Dimmy began. "Papa, we think we know why the visit. Our Rabbi has been arrested! He's an American and they are charging him with subversion!"

Anatole continued, "Subversion for disseminating a false religion. Prayer books, T'fillin, Talleisim, you know, anything not sanctioned by the government! We're trying to get him out before they claim he had an accident. The Rabbi wouldn't eat anything and smuggling food to him is virtually impossible. 'Gifts' and bribes used to work but the door is closed to that. In this climate, his American passport and visa mean nothing to the authorities. Our demonstrations do little but put us in jeopardy and him in more. We need to save him! But how?"

Josef looked at his watch. "I have to leave! I'm surprised at you guys. I thought that the Lubovitchers believe in miracles. Don't they say, 'G-d will help?' Keep in touch! I'll try!"

He simply walked away, no "Good-bye", no hug, no handshake.

IX

The struggle for the preservation of the burial site and her appointment to the librarian job made Maryushka a household name. Watermill now saw her as a person who deserved honor. Her enemies were being punished or relegated to obscurity as her friends became recognized. Still, she had problems. Bureaucracy was no help in solving the critical issues she saw. Happily, the archives were being well established and although the Jewish sources were either dead or emigrated, the information and artifacts were being assembled. The small staff was energized by her spirit and miracles were being performed. Soon the dedication would take place and the town's administration would seek all the credit. She was satisfied that under the circumstances, the work was as good as possible. She was happy to have finished and yearned to get back to her first love, the hospital.

The day of the dedication arrived and a grandstand was erected with banners and signs. She was invited to sit on the dais but declined. Her modest staff decided to sit with her in the audience. Only one thing diminished the joy of the occasion! The news that Mrs. Slomovitch had finally succumbed to the dreaded disease. She sent Josef a long and heartfelt condolence letter. Maryushka had met her several times but her illness had cut the blooming friendship short.

The day of the commemoration was beautiful. The slight breeze set the flags and bunting fluttering. The local and national newspapers all had stories on the occasion but the Watermill press covered it in full as befit it. Miriam took great pains, as she did with all her undertakings, to collect all the pictures and articles in the press. All the dignitaries from Pilski and Watermill were making speeches lauding the achievement and themselves. Finally, the time arrived and Maryushka was introduced with accolades that made her blush. The roar of applause brought Miriam to her feet and she slowly made her way to the podium. The audience settled down after her pleas for them to be seated. She had not prepared a speech. Actually, she had, but no matter what she wrote was not right. She decided to wing it.

In a subdued, emotional tone, she began. "Sons and daughters of Poland! Sisters and brothers of Watermill! The shouts and applause started again! When it subsided she began, "All of the speakers have covered every facet of our reason for being here today. There is little I can add." The PA system kept throwing her words back at her. She paused for a second for the echo to stop. "First, let me ask my team to stand and be recognized." When they rose, a thundering of applause again met them. Maryushka continued, "Now, I want to introduce the other contributors to this magnificent collection that establishes a record of our people's suffering and struggle for freedom in the face of the most brutal man made force against humanity." Everyone looked about! She saw this and responded. "You! Brothers and sisters! You are the ones! Stand up! Applaud yourselves!" And with her arms she coaxed everyone to stand and applaud themselves. She was about to step down when the Mayor took her arm, signaled her to remain on the stage. The photographers popped their flashbulbs at them. The Mayor moved toward to the microphone and raised his arms to invite silence.

"It gives us great pleasure to present you and your staff a certificate of honor for your gift to our city and our people today. With this declaration, we wish to present a medal as Honorary State Librarian." He then placed the medal's ribbon over her head. We would be honored for you to join us by accepting a seat on our town council. We need your wisdom, courage and loyalty on our legislative body." He ended with kisses on both cheeks, as the band broke into the national anthem. Everyone rose and joined in the singing. As soon as it ended, everyone left and Maryushka was alone with her new friends. How would she have time to sit on the council?

Then again, this might be the leverage she needed to push through her hospital agenda. How she wished that Josef could have been there. And that seemed to be the end of her celebrity. One of her opportunities with being on the Town Council would come when she proposed that the old Sloss, the old Watermill landmark, be converted into a museum and archive depository. Immediately, she returned to her post at the hospital and the fight for a newer and bigger one. That Josef was happy for her was no surprise. She knew he would be.

X

The meeting in the hospital and again at their mother's funeral began a new page in the lives of the Slomovitch family. The professor began to realize that there was a terrible void in his life that his students and academic associates could not fill. His sons also began to see the professor in a different light. After the interment, at which his sons said the Kaddish, Josef invited them to his apartment. He was surprised when they removed their boots and sat down on the floor. There was so much he needed to learn from them. They, in turn yearned to learn from him the long past, their roots, their identity.

The conversation over a small snack was about their mother, how terrible it was for her to suffer through her long bout with cancer. How she, as all women in the Soviet Union, had struggled through the terrible war, what she had to do to keep her babies alive. Although she knew that Josef was doing important work in the army, she never knew what or where he was. Obviously, clandestine operations meant no communication. Friends with husbands or sons at the front shared their mail with her, to comfort her in her terrible loneliness. Anatole moved the discussion away from the war. "Papa, you were on duty in Watermill! Isn't that where our family came from? That is before we settled in Moscow?"

"Anatole," the professor began.

"Please call me by my real name, Aaron," the boy interrupted. "And this is David," pointing toward his brother. "Forgive me! Go on!" "And my name is Joseph!" the father answered, reintroducing himself. All burst into laughter. "The last time, you asked me about Maryushka, sorry, Miriam. Well it is from her that my knowledge about Watermill derives. Whatever I learned from my grandfather seems like a 'Once upon a time' fairy tale. Not Peter and the Wolf, but close." He proceeded to tell the Watermill saga, of how their ancestors migrated to this idyllic valley with its castle, the Shloss. The boys were soon entranced with the narration and dared not interrupt. When the part about the romance between the tailor's son and the baron's daughter was starting, Josef paused to set the tea samovar boiling. "They say her hair was black as the crows that flew out of the Shloss. Anatole, that's where you get your hair from. It is interesting that the candlelight signal that the lovers had used was identical to the one we used in the war. And you know, the secret stairway which the lovers escaped through, we were able to make use of that, too."

Dmitri spoke up, after a sip of the steaming tea. "What an unbelievable story. Is it true? Did it really happen?"

"Well, you understand that all this was handed down through many generations. But Maryushka showed me the landmarks. She took me to where Chayele was buried, where the small stone marker remains with her name in Hebrew letters. I saw where the Jews had their businesses, the hardware store, the blacksmith shop, the tavern!"

Anatole begged him to go on, unable to understand his brother's skepticism. But Josef was bothered by Dimmy's remark. "Maybe, some day, I'll take you there and you'll see for yourself As you can see, like all fairy tales this all had a happy ending. And you are it!" He saw that evening was soon approaching and he tried to hurry it up. He skipped the details of the passage to Russia, Baroness Maryushka's conversion but not how her husband the tailor studied to become a rabbi. This impressed them greatly. That was a rabbi in the lineage of their family was a revelation to them. As they were preparing to leave. Dmitri apologized for doubting. Josef threw his arms around him, as tears ran down his cheeks. How he had longed for a moment like this! He silently pledged to himself to keep the family together. He had much to learn from his children and much to teach.

XI

The telephone jumped off the cradle. The professor heard Dmitri's voice at the other end. "It's me Dmitri! How about breakfast?"

Josef had to orient himself to a call this early and especially from his son. "Sure! Where?" To Dmitri's response he gave a simple, "Yes!" and began getting ready, shower and shave. The restaurant was not far from the campus. Josef decided to take public transportation for fear he might be followed in his car. Though he had rushed, Dmitri was already there with one of his friends. "Let's order first," he suggested. "The pastry is especially good!"

The professor asked no questions. Nor were they needed. The urgency in Dmitri's voice was sufficient. "We just got word that the Rabbi is going to be tried and sent to the gulag. His visa and passport have been destroyed and the prosecutor has prepared his case. They say it is not a question of freedom of religion; it is purely foreign intervention in the Soviet society. They had no problem getting the KGB agents to testify. We have to get him out!" That was the whole conversation. The food finished, they left to go their own way. The younger men had no idea if anything would come of this meeting and neither did Josef. He went home and immediately went to his clothes closet. He laid out his uniform and began to dress. The full length mirror proved how fit he still was and helped him adjust the chest full of medals he fixed to his jacket. He was ready to leave and turned to make a phone call. "Dimmy, meet me for lunch!" He waited for no reply except, "Yes!" He had to move quickly to get to his lunch appointment.

The policeman on duty approached him as he parked his car in front of the KGB headquarters but when he saw the medals, he merely saluted and walked away. Josef skipped up the front steps as though he were twenty years younger. Again his medals were saluted at the door, no questions asked. As slyly as he could, he slipped the eye piece over his left eye and marched up to the desk. The KGB man was not impressed. Seated at his desk, he asked, "Your business?"

"Where are your manners, boy?" Josef barked. "You stand to attention when a senior officer approaches! Weren't you in the army?" Apparently the KGB man got the message, jumped to attention and awaited what was to come next. "Where is your commanding officer?" Josef moderated his tone.

The duty officer stuttered, "He will be in later . . . after three or four, sir." Slomovitch barked back, "This business can't wait! Army command cannot wait on a commanding officer that is never at his post!" With this he waved a very official paper in front of the 'B' officer. "We have an order to bring the Rabbi Arba to military headquarters, immediately! Immediately!" The second "Immediately!" sharper than the first. "You have this Arba person in custody, don't you?" The man pulled out a sheaf of papers from his desk, still standing and finally located the name. He nodded and, holding the papers in one hand, reached for the telephone. Josef reached out and grabbed the phone, shouting, "Do you want to compromise national security?" Then he turned around to check if anyone else could hear and in a whisper said, "I'm not supposed to tell anyone but this prisoner is an important double agent and it's secret. Do you understand?"

The expected, "Yes, sir!" led to the next step. "Obviously you cannot leave your post. Is there anyone else that we can trust to carry out this mission?" When the answer was, "No!" Josef persuaded the officer to give him the keys to the cell. The directions to the cell were easy to follow and in no time the confused Rabbi was being spirited out of the building. The duty officer ran to help open the door and saluted as they descended the steps to the car. The policeman was there, eager to help get the man into the back seat. He saluted and wished them a good day, as the car pulled away.

Slomovitch checked his mirrors for any suspicious cars, then sped to his luncheon appointment. He didn't know that shortly after they left, the KGB chief had called in to find out that a one-eyed Vice-Marshall had taken his prize prisoner away. No name. No orders. Nothing! What Josef knew was that totalitarian countries respect authority. The higher, the greater. It was not as easy getting the Rabbi to cooperate. In his bewildered condition he did not respond to this large man in uniform. When Josef told Arba to come with him, that made no sense. The Rabbi was accustomed to KGB men, not a soldier in full uniform. What made the difference was a greeting Miriam had taught him in Watermill. "Shalom Aleichem!"

XII

Everything in Watermill began happening at a rapid pace. Most everybody attributed the change to the miracle worker, the nurse/librarian. Few cared that she had been on trial. The past was gone, the now was what mattered and this woman made it happen. Her position on the council gave her status but it also gave resentment. Her priorities were directed toward the welfare of the people. Her special interests were essential services. The foundation for the new hospital was poured and housing units would be ready for the winter weather. Her phone calls were answered and her mail promptly addressed. She had become a force to be reckoned with. The name Maryushka had become synonymous with "will do." Little did they realize that the problem was little men in big positions.

The call came while she was in conference with her chief of staff. Medical supplies were being funneled to the black market and the culprit had been found. "Hello! Who is calling?" She immediately recognized the voice, although it was weak and muffled by pain. "Mar! Mar!" The Mayor could not muster the strength to say her full name. She motioned to her assistant to the adjacent phone. "Maryushala, I'm going fast! Help us!" Where was he calling from? Home? Office?

"Janosh!" she screamed into the phone, "Where are you?" There was no reply. She ordered the dispatcher to send emergency equipment to his home and office but it was too late. He was slumped over his desk, the phone cradle in his lap where it had fallen. Why had he called her instead of emergency? She had begun to rely on him to support her in the council.

He was like an uncle to her. The only family she had. His last words still rang in her ears. His children were summoned and a state funeral was arranged. He was a devout atheist so no funeral Mass would be held, although the priests were assembled in the front row of the funeral chapel. Many grieved but none as much as Miriam. This was the first personal loss for her since her family were taken away and massacred by the Nazis. He had been a widower for many years and his children had left Watermill for a better life. His children came to console her. The town square was full of people who came to pay their respects. The members of the council each spoke and the Mayor of Pilski gave the eulogy. Maryushka declined to speak and everyone understood. A week of mourning was proclaimed but the construction didn't stop. When the council finally met, it made two decisions. One to name the square Janosh Plaza, and two, to hold elections for Mayor. The ballots were printed. Several members of the council had chosen to run and there were others from other organizations. Miriam was happy with her position on the council and in the hospital. She decided not to endorse any of the candidates but pledged to support the winner.

The week of the election was full off all the hoopla and rhetoric customary in a local competition. No one would have guessed that a train was speeding four passengers on their way to Watermill from Moscow.

XIII

The diesel engine whined as they made their way to the reserved compartment. Even in their privacy, they could not be safe. Whatever was taken had to be stored so as not to raise suspicion. The KGB was the most organized and powerful element of the Soviet system, with spies and patriots everywhere to inform on dissidents or any suspicious activity. Even a moving train was no assurance. After all, it was alerted to the rabbi's activities among the young Jewish students. All the prayer books and articles of faith were confiscated to be used as evidence against the rabbi. Surely their agents would be on this trip. The Polish border would be no protection on a Russian train.

The conductor came through and checked their tickets and travel papers. He asked each of them questions and wanted to know why the fourth man was sleeping during the day? Josef explained that Ivan was medicated against motion sickness. "He has been heaving in the toilet since we left Moscow! Poor man!. We would have flown if my brother was not so allergic. Should I try to wake him up?" Slomovitch asked. The conductor left. The suggestion of illness worked. The trip went on, seemingly uneventful. Caution still demanded that they keep up their vigilance and so one person stayed awake all the time. During the night, the professor held his watch. The Pravda that he found in the cabin held his attention for a little time but there was something that seemed to bother him. During the time he was trying to get Arba out of his cell, the rabbi kept saying, "Thank you Rebbe! Thank you Rebbe" Was it an illusion, the effect that near starvation brings, or the stress of the incarceration? It had never occurred to him that the rabbi actually saw his old dear beloved Lubovitcher Rebbe in the cell, saying, "Shalom Aleichem!" instead of him. Was it possible that for the rabbi there was no Russian officer leading him from captivity? There was only the Rebbe? After all, who else would Ha'Shem have sent to save him?

As the sun rose, the rabbi awoke and went to the washroom to cleanse the sleep from his body. The boys awoke too and immediately followed the ritual. Anatole reached into the closet and drew out his travel bag with his camera equipment. Secreted in side was a small pouch which he handed to the rabbi. No sooner had he opened the drawstring that he said, "Baruch Ha'shem!" over and over. He set the t'fillin on his forehead and his arm. He didn't ask for a Tallis but when Dmitri pulled one out from under his shirt the rabbi began to cry. The boys had to fight to control their own tears. Never had the professor witnessed such a scene. The rabbi turned toward the east and proceeded to make his shacharis prayer. He finished and removed the religious articles and handed them to Dmitri, who proceeded to put them on and say the Morning Prayer also, and then Anatole did the same.

Anatole finished and carefully put the articles away. He knew his father would not know what to do and might be embarrassed if he offered them to him. Perhaps that time would come. Days passed into nights and so on. The passing scenes reminded Josef of the long-ago odyssey when he and Maryushka wandered from Watermill to Moscow. It made him think, of the other escape, of a baroness and a tailor. Every mile was a mile that brought him closer to Watermill. It was his return home, and through circumstances beyond his control he was taking his family there and the Lubovitcher rabbi, too.

XIV

The elections were over and the ballots counted. The scores ran back and forth. None had a majority vote. In fact, all together, they had not garnered a majority. Through no effort on her part, Miriam had been elected Mayor of Watermill. How this happened, she would never understand. How could she decline such an honor? Everyone who voted for her knew her history. She was a Jew! She was a madame! She had been tried for treason! She was a woman Was a Jew! When the men who had run saw the results of the balloting, they declared her unanimously elected by acclimation! The Jewish madame was to be Madam Mayor of Watermill. The old Mayor had begged her in his last breath, "Help us!" Now it would be her job. Everyone on the council pledged their support. Even those who doubted felt that it was a sign. The plans for inauguration were made up. Dignitaries from as far away as Warsaw were planning to attend. Arrangements had to be made to accommodate the guests. Not since before the war had this province had such a gala affair being planned. Maryushka had planned to open a new hospital but that it was not ready, was obvious. She would find time to keep her eye on its construction despite her mayoral duties. She called Moscow to tell Josef the news but received no answer. She wanted so much to share it with him. With all the miracles that were coming her way, she was afraid that some evil might come to destroy her happiness.

The phone rang several times before she was able to reach it. "I was about to give up again!" the voice at the other end chided. Josef sounded like he was next door. "I've been calling since Warsaw! You're never in! Where on earth . . ."

"Josef darling! Where are you? My calls to your apartment have never gotten through."

"We're in Pilski! I can practically see the Shloss! We missed the connection and will have to wait overnight or rent a car. Should we wait?" He had heard the "Darling!" but pretended not to.

"Don't wait! You'll miss everything! Do you have the boys with you? I'll keep dinner warm! Twenty miles! Hurry!" He had no choice; she hung up before he could decide. He turned toward his group and shrugged his shoulders, marched over to the car rental and loaded everyone into a late model van. The clerk asked if he could use a guide map. His reply was a big laugh. As they reached the crest of the hill, the sun was setting just as it had the day a Jew and his pregnant wife, Sarah first saw Watermill. The rabbi asked Josef to stop for a minute so he could make the afternoon prayer, just as Shlomo had done. This time no four horsemen bothered them. His two sons joined in the prayers as Josef waited in the van. Silently they returned to their seats and continued on their way. The van sped around the curve where a blind Nazi officer met his fate. "One day, I'll tell you about this curve," he shouted to his sons, over the rush of wind. "Look ahead to your right!" he called out. The castle of Watermill stood guard over the valley, their valley. The awesome sight made the boys speechless, while the rabbi kept repeating, "Baruch Ha'Shem!"

Josef realized that everything had changed since he left. Everything except the Shloss. He stopped a Pole to ask directions. "No problem!" came the reply. "Are you here for the inauguration?" Then he gave directions to Maryushka's place. In a moment the welcome would be complete. The door to her apartment was open but he knocked anyway. The boys hesitated; the rabbi saw no mezuzah on the door and also hesitated, but Josef flew into Miriam's open arms. They separated as soon as she realized that the others were standing awkwardly waiting at the door. She began to apologize in Polish then switched to Russian. Josef introduced Dmitri and Anatole, completely forgetting that they preferred their new identity. ". . . and this is our dear rabbi, Rabbi Arba. It's a long story but we're starving."

The men took turns in the washroom and returned to the modest dining area. Her apartment was utilitarian, modern and simple, even though she had a prestigious position as head nurse and a seat on the town council, How they would manage would be a problem, but not considering what they had gone through. The boys sat watching Miriam and their father going over old times, new times, and in-between times. At times it was completely confusing to them.

There would be a time after the inauguration for Marushka to tell them the whole story of Watermill. The rabbi just sat there as though he was in another world. Finally, he spoke. Up to this point he obeyed Josef and never uttered a word, except to pray and say, "Baruch Ha'Shem!"

"What is my mission? I have a mission! I must contact my Rebbe and let him know . . ." His voice trailed off into silence as he broke into tears. "My mission! My mission!" he murmured.

The boys hugged him. They tried to comfort him. "G-d will help! The Rebbe will help!" and finally, "Papa will help!" They forgot that Josef was in a foreign country, illegally! Maryushka saw the danger and the opportunity. She would use her influence as best she could, after tomorrow. Then Josef remembered the young Pole's question. "What inaugural?"

In all the excitement, Miriam had forgotten to tell them. Tomorrow was the day she was to be inducted as the Mayor of Watermill. And they would be her guests!

Not the way they looked! As soon as they turned in for the night she got busy making calls. The haberdasher reopened his shop. The shoe store, the hat shop, all got busy to help. Early the next morning, a stack of boxes appeared before her apartment door. Another miracle. The sun had also risen, bright and cheerful for the celebration day. The rabbi and the boys started with their wash, their prayer and breakfast. Miriam was impressed with this ritual, which she had not seen since her grandfather passed away. Josef helped with the clothing, amazed that she had estimated their sizes perfectly. To his compliment she laughed, "I just pictured you all lying naked in a hospital bed! All except the rabbi, of course!"

By eleven o'clock they were ready to take their seats at the ceremony. The square was jammed with people. The band was playing mazurkas, polkas and waltzes along with the usual Polish marches. All the dignitaries had already taken their seats as befit their positions. The front-row seats were reserved for honored guests. One of the late night calls arranged for Josef and his people. She took his arm as they proudly came down the aisle. She couldn't decide if having him there was more important than the inauguration itself. The clock in the town hall tower chimed the half hour and the President of the council rose to the lectern. "Would Marushka Aragon please join us on the dais!" The band broke into ruffles and flourishes as she stood and made her way. A deafening applause drowned out the music. Soon after she sat down, the audience got quiet and the speeches began. Speech upon-speeches; History lessons! Poetic renditions! The war years! World War I and World War II! The Mayor of Pilski, the county seat, spoke briefly, as did the representative from Warsaw. Finally, the President of the Council introduced the honoree. He glorified her virtues, lauded her tenacity, praised her accomplishments, applauded her heroism and skipped the trial and accusations that almost ruined her and her friends. "Our first and most gracious lady mayor, Maryushka Miriam Aragon."

She stood as the band struck up the Hatikvah. Well, gracious as she was, the thought entered her mind, "was this a prank or a sincere expression of her being a Jew? No doubt, it was a surprise! From her smile one would never guess the turmoil that surged within her. The music stopped but the accolade from the people didn't. She had time to settle down. She had time to see the anthem was an appreciation of who she was. It made her proud. She had glanced toward her guests and saw the rabbi and Josef's sons singing the words. Now she signaled the audience for silence and it begrudgingly came.

"My dear brothers and sisters, honored guests on the dais, special friends," she humbly began. "I hope someone is on duty at the hospital!" A roar of laughter rippled across the plaza. "I take this oath of office as sincerely as I have accepted all of my responsibilities. I pledge on my honor that I will serve the cause of truth, right and freedom to my best. Whenever needed, just come to me. The first official act I will make is to remove the door to the Mayor's office." A roar rose from the crowd. What they had heard from the other speakers was rhetoric. They knew her words were true. "I need to thank you all for entrusting me with this grave position. I need to thank our dear mayor, Janosh, who decided to put me on the council, who supported our fight with the bureaucracy, whom we will all miss. And I must thank the most important person of all. The man who served us through the Red Army, who is really a son of Watermill. Who risked his own life to save ours! Let us welcome him home! Vice-Marshal Professor Josef Slomovitch!"

The audience rose as one, with cheers and applause. Josef stood and walked to the platform as the band struck up the Soviet national anthem. He climbed the steps to be greeted with handshakes and hugs. Finally, the most important hug of all. His welcome home hug. His return home hug! And Maryushka didn't want to let go! Even as 'the Polish national anthem' played. What a happy ending to the Watermill Saga!

XV

The crowds dispersed, and the dignitaries disappeared. That Maryushka had been sworn in was a fact that none of them planned for or agreed with. They would have to live with it, but Miriam had different ideas. She knew that the council would thwart her ideas and oppose her programs but that problem would wait for another day. First and foremost was the need to repatriate the rabbi. Strings had to be pulled and now that she had an official title, it would be easier. At least that's what she thought. She called Mr. Bureaucracy in Warsaw and was put on hold. Well, this hold lasted several days. When the return call finally came she was advised to write the Office of State for the appropriate forms etc., etc. At first Miriam was calm but firm, but when the papers did not arrive, she begun to vent her spleen. "This is not the mayor's secretary, you buffoon! This is the mayor! I have been patient and now I demand action." No Janosh was she. The phone line sizzled. The next voice sounded more official and she repeated her request. The sticky wheels started to move and she was advised the necessary papers would get to her the next day. To the question, "With whom am I speaking?" she received the name of the head of the immigration and passport department.

With the morning mail, the appropriate material arrived and she set about to arrange for the rabbi's return to the United States. Josef explained that this was a visit and that he and his sons had to return home, too. He could not leave the job without officially terminating it and that his time to retire was only a few short years away. The boys were sure that Watermill was a nice place but they too had responsibility to finish their schooling and work in JRM. As Madam Mayor, Miriam's offer to have an open-door policy was taken seriously and her office was full of people the very next day, seeking help. She apologized to her guests from Moscow but what could she do except fulfill her pledge.

The tour of the town did not take long. Josef's memory was keen, and with the Shloss as his compass he was able to take the rabbi and his sons to the important landmarks. The construction was under way, but the places that he knew were clear in his mind. He pointed out the place where the old synagogue stood, had been burned to the ground with the congregation inside, where the original homes of the Jewish settlers were before the big fire. He made everything come to life in their minds. They approached the gravesite of a baby called, Chayele and bent down to read the worn words. The rabbi pointed out the Hebrew letters, "P N" which were the Hebrew abbreviations for 'here is buried'. He then led the boys in the Kaddish. The "Yisgadal V'Yiskadash . . ." seemed to hang in the air, for all the years the prayer had not been said. This was his blood, his family over which his sons were saying the memorial prayer. Josef stood silently, the tears flowing from his eyes. Then they moved over to where the flattening mound of the slaughtered lay, and repeated the Kaddish. Thanks to Miriam, there would soon be a memorial park where they stood. As they left the rabbi repeated over and over again, Aleichem Hashalom! "Peace be with them!"

The highlight of the tour of course was the Shloss, the baron's castle where his ancestors found each other, found danger, found rescue and undying love. Undying love! Slomovitch had a strange feeling as he explained all the details of his own time in the Shloss as a German officer. He pointed out the doors, that big wooden door that the baron had sealed to bury his errant daughter, and the front door from which he made his exit, where Helga watched the blind Kolonel jump into the car and drive away with Maryushka. The dining hall that he seldom used, the General's office and then the stairway that led to the room.

Anatole found it difficult to navigate and asked; "How did you manage?"

Josef laughed, "It wasn't easy! Close your eyes and pretend you are blind. But remember, I was with intelligence and was trained. They told me exactly how many stairs there were. The room at the top was more of a problem. After I became accustomed to the layout it was easier."

Dmitri said, "But Dad, you could really see!"

"That's just the thing, Dimmy, It was essential for the mission's success that I be totally blind, not just pretend blind. Here's the desk just as I left it." He bent over to blow a cloud of dust off the surface. He walked around and sat down in his chair. It felt much larger than he imagined it would. He leaned back, his head resting on the leather, his memory feeling Helga's fingers running through his hair. An involuntary smile crossed is face.

"What?" Asked Anatole.

"Nothing!" he answered. "Was thinking in German! Here's where I stowed the radio gear." Going over to the secret alcove that the boys would have never found on their own. The wireless was still intact but the wires were strewn about. "Whoever found these after I left was pretty angry. This is the window that we used to signal each other. Everyone thought it meant for Maryushka to come up for monkey business when all we did was spy business. Here, take this spot of wax as a souvenir. This same candle could have been used by the baroness to signal her lover, the tailor's son. Now to the most important part. The secret stairway! If not for this, the governess would have not been able to save the young lovers. Maryushka and I wouldn't have been able to meet secretly and we wouldn't be here today!" They climbed down the secret stairway completely in the dark, feeling each other to guide themselves down. Josef pushed at the door but it wouldn't budge. He asked the boys to help but it wouldn't move. They had to turn and climb the jet-black stairwell again. The secret door at the top didn't give way at first. No one said it but it crossed their minds that they could have been entombed in that stairway and died. What a twist of fate that would have been!

It gave way and they realized that the misty air of the Shloss was too much, so they decided not to examine the crypt. Besides that, it would have been awkward for the rabbi to be in the room with the Christian altars, coffins and crucifixes. As they walked back to the center of town, they sucked in the warm spring air that Watermill offered them. This was not an industrial town and except for the construction dust and noise, it remained as idyllic as their ancestors had found it. The boys couldn't wait to tell Maryushka of their adventure.

The dinner at a local dairy restaurant was like home cooked. Actually it was home cooked. The perogi and blini were mouth-melting delicious. But the boys weren't interested in the food. Each interrupted the other, fighting for the next line. The discomfort they felt talking with her melted away as laughter caressed their every word. She had a hard time adding her own input, their enthusiasm was so great. Then came the blockbuster.

"Is it true that you are going to make the Shloss into a museum? Dimmy started. Before he could finish, Anatole jumped in:

"Why not advertise it as Museum and Haunted Castle? You know the story of the baron, the baroness, the daughter, the rejected betrothal and so on. On the ground floor the War Museum and Memorial. Then a guided tour of the crypt and the stairway to the room where the heavy wooden door sealed the fate of the lovers. And another guide dressed as the girl's nurse could lead the people through the secret dark escape to the outside door. You could sell souvenirs and stuff"

"Make a fortune! Watermill would become famous!" added Anatole again.

"You know, I need two brilliant young aides in my office! Miriam offered.

She could see the message in Josef's eyes. "We have to go back! That doesn't mean that we can't return, but the boys must finish school and I have time before I retire. But that is not too far in the future. Actually, I hope you can wait, Madam Mayor. The papers are being processed and we will get the rabbi on a flight from Warsaw to the U.S. and us to Moscow. But let's not spoil the celebration." He had ordered a bottle of shlivovitz in honor of the occasion:

The rabbi made a special blessing and all added, "Amen!" For the first time he joined in the conversation. "This is a real "mashka!" Everyone was surprised to see him gulp it down. "The Rebbe's favorite!" The warmth that the drink brought gave him the strength to talk to the boys. "Dovidl and Aaron" he began. His affectionate use of their names was very touching. "That I have to leave my responsibility is painful, indeed, but leaving you, children, is unbearable! But this is the will of Ha'Shem and the Rebbe. Another will take my place and you will go back to the mission and the danger." He paused, then reached for the young sons of Slomovitch and said the Hebrew invocation. "May the Lord bless you and keep you! May the Lord shine." Remember that Ha'Shem is with you, always. Remember that you are the Rebbe's sons! I will pray for you!" These were the last words they would hear from the rabbi. When they left for the airport in Warsaw, he didn't say goodbye or even "Shalom!" He never said "Thank you!" to Miriam or Josef but he didn't have to: Miriam and Josef had arranged everything. Miriam accompanied them to the airport to be sure everything was in order. She kissed and hugged the boys and ordered them to return. The boys walked away when she threw her arms around Josef. The kisses.wet with tears. would be private between them. They had returned home and she believed they would again. Now she had a job to do. In the name of all those who had lived and died, she had a job to do! She swore that Watermill would not die as the town of Dobromil had.

Epilogue

AS IDYLLIC AS Watermill was, nothing ran as smootly as one would have hoped for. Resentment and animosity were ingredients that entered into every situation and anti-Semitism was never far from the surface. Fox's henchmen used all their power to get his sentence overturned. As the mayor, Miriam fought for her people but in the face of time and obstruction, her dreams for the memorial park and hospital both lay on the drawing board, forever. Any and all faults or delays were laid at her open door and her heroic deeds were all but forgotten. That the housing was completed before the most severe winter in decades, was a victory but not attributed to her but rather to the system. From the Lubovitcher Rabbi, she recieved a note of thanks and a gold Star of David. Josef's mail, detailed the problems he and the boys had encountered on their return. Return to Watermill, on indefinite hold. The Shloss museum was going to go forward according to plan. It would be a shrine! A monument to Watermill's past.

EM

Edwards Brothers Malloy
Thorofare, NJ USA
May 14, 2013